Irrigation and Water Management for Sustainable Crop Production

NIPA® GENX ELECTRONIC RESOURCES & SOLUTIONS P. LTD.
New Delhi-110 034

About the Author

Dr. Sunil Kumar is presently working as Assistant Professor-cum-Junior Scientist in the Department of Agronomy, BAU Sabour. He has completed his B.Sc. (Ag) from B.H.U., Varanasi and M.Sc. (Ag) in Agrometeorology from Govind Ballabh Pant University of Agriculture and Technology, Pantnagar. He has completed his Ph.D. in Agrometeorology and Environmental Sciences from SHUATS, Prayagraj, U.P. He has availed ICAR-JRF in Physical Sciences for pursuing his M.Sc. (Ag) and CSIR-JRF in Earth Atmosphere, Ocean and Planetary Sciences. He was given Young Scientist Award for outstanding contribution in 2017 by Society for Agriculture Innovation and Development (SAID), Ranchi (Jharkhand), India. He received Excellence in Teaching Award for outstanding contribution in Teaching in 2018. He has been actively involved in teaching, research and extension at BAU Sabour since 2012. He is Editor of the Journal of Agricultural Extension and Rural economics and Associate Editor of the Journal, Advances in agricultural Technology and Plant Sciences. He has published more than hundred publications as research papers in national and international journals of repute, book chapters etc. including five books. He has also a significant contribution in the field of Aerosol and its impact on Crop productivity, Crop Simulation, climate change, Agromet Advisory Services, Remote Sensing and GIS at Bihar Agricultural University, Sabour.

Irrigation and Water Management for Sustainable Crop Production

Sunil Kumar

Assistant Professor cum Junior Scientist
Department of Agronomy
Bihar Agricultural University
Sabour, Bihar, India

NIPA® GENX ELECTRONIC RESOURCES & SOLUTIONS P. LTD.

New Delhi-110 034

NIPA® GENX ELECTRONIC RESOURCES & SOLUTIONS P. LTD.

101,103, Vikas Surya Plaza, CU Block
L.S.C. Market, Pitam Pura, New Delhi-110 034
Ph : +91-11-43860225, Mob.: +91 9717133558, 9540816132
E-mail: newindiapublishingagency@gmail.com
Website: www.nipaersources.com

Print ISBN: 978-93-58873-00-9
ebook ISBN: 978-93-58879-84-1

NIPA® also publishes books in a variety of electronic formats. Some content that appears in print may not be available in electronic books, and vice versa.

Composed and Designed by NIPA®.

Preface

Water is the most precious gift of the nature and it is also the most crucial element for sustainability of the life in the earth. India's total water consumption alone is the higher than any other continents. The Agricultural sector is the largest consumer of water followed by the domestic sector and the industrial sector. This book addresses several aspects of water scarcity and its management to save the world and for a sustainable life. It discusses about irrigation water quality and criteria to determine water quality. It covers management issues and soil responses to the use of irrigation water of varying quality. To make the best use of water for agriculture and to improve water productivity, it needs to adopt modern efficient irrigation method. Drip and sprinkler irrigation is a solution that reduces conveyance and distribution losses and allows higher water use efficiency. One of the chapters discusses about drip irrigation in detail. Due to over exploitation of ground water and erratic nature of monsoon, there has been depletion of ground water across the world. It is discussed here in this book about the ground water and its proper use.

This book emphasizes about the wastewater which must be treated to ensure a safe environment and foster public health. Effluent which meets set discharge standards can be appropriately used for aquaculture and also irrigation. This book highlights different types of droughts and their management. In addition, this book also combines the latest information on water stress and frequently encountered abiotic stress in the terrestrial surface. Its deleterious effects on plant growth and productivity. This book further discusses the strategies to improve the agriculture, especially in the climate change situation.

The book is a resourceful read for students, teachers, and readers including engineers and researchers in water technology.

Author

Contents

1

Irrigation, Water Quality and Management

1.1 Introduction

Water scarcity is seen as a major constraint to intensify agriculture in a sustainable manner as an attempt to meet the food requirements of a rapidly growing human population. The ever-increasing human population, climate change due to increased emissions of greenhouse gases (GHGs), and intensification of agriculture, are putting severe pressure on the world's two major non-renewable resources of soil and water, and thus pose a big challenge to produce sufficient food to meet the current food demand. The present world population of 7.3 billion people is predicted to grow to over 9 billion by 2050, with the majority of this population increase occurring in developing countries, most of which already face food shortages. A 70% increase in current agricultural productivity will be required to produce sufficient food if these human population growth predictions prove to be correct. In this context, concerted efforts are being made globally to improve the effectiveness of water which will be used for enhancing the production of irrigated crops. Additionally, efforts are also being made to improve water harvesting and water conservation in rain-fed agriculture.

The injudicious use of saline/brackish water is all too often associated with the development of soil salinity, sodicity, ion toxicity, and groundwater pollution. Because of these negative effects, it is important to have a better understanding of exactly how the quality of water influences the management of irrigated agriculture, especially in arid and semi-arid regions.

Salinity, sodicity and ion toxicity are major problems in irrigation waters. In arid areas, where rainfall does not adequately leach salts from the soil, an accumulation of salts will occur in the crop's root-zone. Thus, periodic testing of soils and waters is required to monitor any change in salt content. Sodicity, the presence of excess sodium, will result in a deterioration of the soil structure, thereby reducing water penetration into and through the soil. Toxicity refers to the critical concentration of some salts such as chloride, boron, sodium and some trace elements, above which plant growth is adversely affected by those salts.

This chapter addresses several aspects of irrigation water quality and criteria to determine water quality. It will also cover management issues and soil responses to the use of irrigation water of varying quality. The information presented in this chapter is an updated and improved version of an excerpt from an earlier irrigation water quality manual (Shahid 2004).

1.2 Quality of Irrigation Water

The concentration and composition of soluble salts in water will determine its quality for various purposes (human and livestock drinking, irrigation of crops, etc.). The quality of water is, thus, an important component with regard to sustainable use of water for irrigated agriculture, especially when salinity development is expected to be a problem in an irrigated agricultural area.

There are four basic criteria for evaluating water quality for irrigation purposes:

- Total content of soluble salts (salinity hazard)
- Relative proportion of sodium (Na+) to calcium ($Ca^{2+)}$ and magnesium (Mg^{2+}) ions – sodium adsorption ratio (sodium hazard) 114 5 Irrigation Water Quality
- Residual sodium carbonates (RSC) – bicarbonate (HCO_3) and carbonate (CO_3) anions concentration, as it relates to Ca^{2+} plus Mg^{2+} ions.
- Excessive concentrations of elements that cause an ionic imbalance in plants or plant toxicity.

In order to achieve the first three important criteria, the following characteristics need to be determined in the irrigation waters: electrical conductivity (EC), soluble anions (CO^{3-} HCO_3 , Cl and SO_4) where Cl and SO_4 are optional and soluble cations (Na^+ , K^+ , Ca_2^+, Mg^{2+}) where K is optional. Finally, boron level must also be measured. The pH of the irrigation water is not an acceptable criterion of water quality because the water pH tends to be buffered by the soil, and most crops can tolerate a wide pH range. A detailed description of the techniques commonly employed for the analysis of irrigation water is available.

1.3 Salinity Hazard

The most influential water quality guideline on crop productivity is the water salinity hazard as measured by electrical conductivity (ECw). The primary effect of high ECw water on crop productivity is the inability of the plant to compete with ions in the soil solution for water (physiological drought). The higher the EC, the less water is available to plants, even though the soil may appear wet. Because plants can only transpire "pure" water, usable plant water in the soil solution decreases dramatically as EC increases.

The amount of water transpired through a crop is directly related to yield; therefore, irrigation water with high ECw reduces yield potential (Table 1.2). Actual yield reductions from irrigating with high EC water varies substantially. Factors influencing yield reductions include soil type, drainage, salt type, irrigation system and management. Beyond effects on the immediate crop is the long term impact of salt loading through the irrigation water. Water with an ECw of 1.15 dS/m contains approximately 2,000 pounds of salt for every acre foot of water. You can use conversion factors in Table 1.3 to make this calculation for other water EC levels.

Other terms that laboratories and literature sources use to report salinity hazard are: salts, salinity, electrical conductivity (ECw), or total dissolved solids (TDS). These terms are all comparable and all quantify the amount of dissolved "salts" (or ions, charged particles) in a water sample. However, TDS is a direct measurement of dissolved ions and EC is an indirect measurement of ions by an electrode.

Although people frequently confuse the term "salinity" with common table salt or sodium chloride (NaCl), EC measures salinity from all the ions dissolved in a sample. This includes negatively charged ions (e.g., Cl^{-}, NO^{-3}) and positively charged ions (e.g., Ca^{++}, Na^{+}). Another common source of confusion is the variety of unit systems used with ECw. The preferred unit is deci siemens per meter (dS/m), however millimhos per centimetre (mmho/cm) and micromhos per centimetre (µmho/cm) are still frequently used.

Table 1.1: Salinity hazard of irrigation water (Follett and Soltanpour 2002; Bauder *et al.* 2011)

Hazard	**Dissolved salt content**	
	ppm EC	**(µS cm^{-1})**
None – Water for which no detrimental effects will usually be noticed.	500	750
Some – Water that may have detrimental effects on sensitive crops	500–1000	750–1500
Moderate – Water that may have adverse effects on many crops, thus requiring careful management practices.	1000–2000	1500–3000
Severe – Water that can be used for salt tolerant plants on permeable soils with careful management practices.	2000–5000	3000–7500

1.4 Sodium Hazard

Although plant growth is primarily limited by the salinity (ECw) level of the irrigation water, the application of water with a sodium imbalance can further reduce yield under certain soil texture conditions. Reductions in water infiltration can occur when irrigation water contains high sodium relative to the calcium and magnesium contents. This condition, termed "sodicity," results from excessive soil accumulation of sodium. Sodic water is not the same as saline water. Sodicity causes swelling and dispersion of soil clays, surface crusting and pore plugging. This degraded soil structure condition in turn obstructs infiltration and may increase runoff. Sodicity causes a decrease in the downward movement of water into and through the soil, and actively growing plants roots may not get adequate water, despite pooling of water on the soil surface after irrigation.

The most common measure to assess sodicity in water and soil is called the Sodium Adsorption Ratio (SAR). The SAR defines sodicity in terms of the relative concentration of sodium (Na) compared to the sum of calcium (Ca) and magnesium (Mg) ions in a sample. The SAR assesses the potential for infiltration problems due to a sodium imbalance in irrigation water.

Continued use of water with a high SAR value leads to a breakdown in the physical structure of the soil, a situation caused by excessive amounts of adsorbed sodium on soil colloids. This breakdown in the soil physical structure, results in the dispersion of soil clay and that causes the soil to become hard and compact when dry, and increasingly impervious to water penetration (due to dispersion and swelling) when wet. Fine textured soils, those high in clay, are especially subject to this action. When the concentration of sodium becomes excessive (in proportion to calcium plus magnesium), the soil is said to be sodic. If calcium and magnesium are the predominant cations adsorbed onto the soil exchange complex, the soil can be easily tilled and will have a readily permeable granular structure.

The potential soil infiltration and permeability problems created from applications of irrigation water with high "sodicity" cannot be adequately assessed on the basis of the SAR alone. This is because the swelling potential of low salinity (ECw) water is greater than high ECw waters at the same sodium content (Table 1.4). Therefore, a more accurate evaluation of the infiltration/ permeability hazard requires using the electrical conductivity (ECw) together with the SAR.

Many factors including soil texture, organic matter, cropping system, irrigation system and management affect how sodium in irrigation water affects soils. Soils most likely to show reduced infiltration and crusting from water with elevated SAR (greater than 6) are those containing more than 30% expansive (smectite) clay. Soils containing more than 30% clay include most soils in the clay loam, silty clay loam textural classes and finer and some sandy clay loams.

1.5 Carbonates and Bicarbonates Concentration

Waters high in carbonates (CO_3^{-2}) and bicarbonates (HCO_3) will tend to precipitate calcium carbonate ($CaCO_3$) and magnesium carbonate ($MgCO_3$), when the soil solution becomes concentrated through evapotranspiration. This means that the SAR value will increase, and the relative proportion of sodium ions will become greater. This situation, in turn, will increase the sodium hazard of the soil-water to a level greater than indicated by the SAR value.

1.6 Specific Ion Effects (Toxic Elements)

In addition to salinity and sodium hazards, certain crops may be sensitive to the presence of moderate to high concentrations of specific ions in the irrigation waters or soil solution. Many trace elements are toxic to plants at very low concentrations. Both soil and water testing can help to discover any constituents that might be toxic. Direct toxicity to crops may result from some specific chemical elements in irrigation water, e.g. boron, chloride, and sodium are potentially toxic to plants. The actual concentration of an element in water that will cause toxic symptoms varies, depending on the crop.

When an element is added to the soil through irrigation, it may be inactivated by chemical reactions. Alternatively, it may buildup in the soil until it reaches a toxic level. An element at a given concentration in water may be immediately toxic to a crop, or, it may require a number of years to accumulate in the soil before it becoming toxic.

1.6.1 Sodium Toxicity

Sodium toxicity can occur in the form of leaf burn, leaf scorch and dead tissues running along the outside edges of leaves. In contrast, Cl toxicity is often seen at the extreme leaf tip. In tree crops, a sodium concentration (in excess of 0.25–0.5%) in the leaf tissue is often considered to be a toxic level of sodium. Correct diagnoses can be made from soil, water and plant tissue analysis.

Three levels of exchangeable sodium percentage (ESP) (FAO-UNESCO 1973; Pearson 1960; Abrol 1982), which correspond to three tolerance levels, are defined as: sensitive (ESP < 15), semi-tolerant (ESP 15–40) and tolerant (ESP > 40). The crops/plants listed as sensitive include, among others, beans, maize, peas, orange, peach, mung bean, mash, lentil, gram and cowpea. Semi-tolerant plants include carrot, clover, lettuce, berseem, oat, onion, radish, rye, sorghum, spinach, tomato, and tolerant plants include alfalfa, barley, beet, Rhoades grass and Karnal (Kallar) grass.

1.6.2 Boron Toxicity

Boron is essential to the normal growth of all plants, but the amount required is low. If it exceeds a certain level of tolerance depending on the crop, then boron may cause injury. The range between deficiency and toxicity of boron for many crops is narrow.

In order to sustain an adequate supply of boron to the plant at least 0.02 ppm of boron in the irrigation water may be required. However, to avoid toxicity, boron levels in irrigation water should, ideally, be lower than 0.3 ppm. Higher concentrations of boron will likely require that the intended crop type must first be evaluated with respect to its boron tolerance. Although boron toxicity is not a problem in most areas, it can be an important irrigation water quality parameter. Interestingly, plants grown in soils high in lime may tolerate higher levels of boron than those grown in non-calcareous soils.

Boron is weakly adsorbed by soils. Thus, its actual root-zone concentration may not vary in direct proportion to the degree that boron sourced from the irrigation water has been concentrated in the plant during growth. Symptoms of boron injury may include characteristic leaf 'burning', chlorosis and necrosis, although some boron sensitive species do not develop obvious symptoms. Boron toxicity symptoms first appear on older leaves as yellowing, spotting, or drying of leaf tissues at the tips and edges. The drying and chlorosis often progresses toward the center of the leaf, between the veins as boron accumulates over time (Ayers and Westcot, 1985).

Irrigation water with boron >1.0 ppm may cause toxicity in boron sensitive crops. Table 1.2 describes the effects of a range of boron concentrations in irrigation water on crops (Bauder *et al.* 2011). The relative tolerance of plants to boron is shown in Table 1.3.

Boron levels that have developed in the soil water (saturation extract of soils) through irrigation can have a range of effects on crop yields. Wilcox (1960) presented three classes of crops with regard to boron toxicity: tolerant (2-4 ppm), semi-tolerant (1-2 ppm), and sensitive (0.3-1 ppm). Fruit crops are among the most boron sensitive, and yields of citrus and some stone fruit species are decreased by boron even at soil solution concentrations less than 0.5 ppm.

Table 1.2: Effects of boron (B) concentration in irrigation water on crops (Follett and Soltanpour, 2002; Bauder *et al.* 2011)

Boron concentration (ppm)	Effect on crops
< 0.5	Satisfactory for all crops
0.5–1.0	Satisfactory for most crops
1.0–2.0	Satisfactory for semi-tolerant crops
2.0–4.0	Satisfactory for tolerant crops only

Table 1.3: Relative tolerance of plants to Boron concentration (ppm) in irrigation water (cf. Ludwick *et al.* 1990; Ayers and Westcot, 1985)

Very sensitive (< 0.5 ppm)	Sensitive (0.5–0.75 ppm)	Less sensitive (0.75–1.0 ppm)	Moderately sensitive (1.0–2.0 ppm)	Moderately tolerant (2.0–4.0 ppm)	Tolerant (4.0–6.0 ppm)	Very tolerant (> 6.0 ppm)
Lemon	Avocado	Garlic	Pepper	Lettuce	Tomato	Cotton
Blackberry	Grapefruit	Sweet potato	Pea	Cabbage	Parsley	Asparagus
	Orange	Sunflower	Carrot	Celery	Beet	
	Apricot	Bean	Radish	Turnip		
	Peach	Sesame	Potato	Oats		
	Cherry	Strawberry	Cucumber	Corn		
	Plum	Kidney bean		Clover		
	Grape	Peanut		Squash		
	Walnut			Muskmelon		
	Onion					

1.6.3 Chloride Toxicity

The most common crop toxicity is caused by chlorides in irrigation water. The chloride (Cl) anion occurs in all waters; chlorides are soluble and leach readily to drainage water. Chlorides are necessary for plant growth, though in high concentrations they can inhibit plant growth, and can be highly toxic to some plant species. Water must, thus, be analyzed for Cl concentration when assessing water quality. Table 1.4 shows Cl levels in irrigation water and the effects of Cl on crops. In sensitive crops, symptoms occur when Cl levels accumulate in leaves (0.3-1.0% on a dry weight basis). Ayers and Westcot (1985) reported that Cl toxicity on plants appears first at the leaf tips (which is a very common symptom for chloride toxicity), and progresses from the leaf tip back along the edges as severity of the toxic effect increases. Excessive necrosis is often accompanied by early leaf drop or even total plant defoliation.

Table 1.4: Chloride (Cl^{-1}) levels of irrigation waters and their effects on crops (cf. Ludwick *et al.* 1990; Bauder *et al.* 2011)

Cl^- concentration		Effect on crops
meq l^{-1}	**ppm**	
< 2	< 70	Generally safe for all plants
2–4	70–140	Sensitive plants usually show slight to moderate injury
4–10	141–350	Moderately tolerant plants usually show slight to substantial injury
> 10	> 350	Can cause severe problems

1.6.4 Sulphate

The sulphate ion is a major contributor to salinity in many of Colorado irrigation waters. As with boron, sulphate in irrigation water has fertility benefits, and irrigation water in Colorado often has enough sulphate for maximum production for most crops. Exceptions are sandy fields with

1.6.5 Nitrogen

Nitrogen in irrigation water (N) is largely a fertility issue, and nitrate-nitrogen (NO3 -N) can be a significant N source in the South Platte, San Luis Valley, and parts of the Arkansas River basins. The nitrate ion often occurs at higher concentrations than ammonium in irrigation water. Waters high in N can cause quality problems in crops such as barley and sugar beets and excessive vegetative growth in some vegetables. However, these problems can usually be overcome by good fertilizer and irrigation management. Regardless of the crop, nitrate should be credited toward the fertilizer rate especially when the concentration exceeds 10 ppm NO_3^-. Table 3 provides conversions from ppm to pounds per acre inch.

1.7 pH and Alkalinity

The acidity or basicity of irrigation water is expressed as pH (< 7.0 acidic; > 7.0 basic). The normal pH range for irrigation water is from 6.5 to 8.4. Abnormally low pH's are not common in Colorado, but may cause accelerated irrigation system corrosion where they occur. High pH's above 8.5 are often caused by high bicarbonate (HCO_3^-) and carbonate (CO_3^{2-}) concentrations, known as alkalinity. High carbonates cause calcium and magnesium ions to form insoluble minerals leaving sodium as the dominant ion in solution. As described in the sodium hazard section, this alkaline water could intensify the impact of high SAR water on sodic soil conditions. Excessive bicarbonate concentrates can also be problematic for drip or micro-spray irrigation systems when calcite or scale build up causes reduced flow rates through orifices or emitters. In these situations, correction by injecting sulfuric or other acidic materials into the system may be required.

1.8 Irrigation water management

Irrigation water management means the proper control of water being distributed to minimize losses that could cause degradation of water quantity and quality as well as the proper application of water on fields as the crop needs dictate. Thus, seepage from distribution systems is controlled, irrigation water is applied in a timely manner and over irrigation is avoided.

1.9 Scheme wide considerations

Good irrigation water management involves control of seepage from reservoirs and canals as these water wastes can create problems with high water tables adjacent to the works and on low lands in and near the schemes. High water tables in arid and semi-arid climatic zones will move excessive saline water to root zones and water tables thus causing water quality problems.

1.10 Field considerations

Irrigation water management within farm fields requires careful timing of water application to be certain the crop water requirements are met but not exceeded. Excessive water applications not only waste water but provide the flows to move agricultural chemicals or other elements that under some conditions become toxic, from the crop o~ crop root zone where they can be used by the plants to ground water aquifers or high water table areas where they are usually considered pollutants.

1.11 Agronomic practices

Agronomic practices in irrigated areas can also impact water quality. Pest control for example can greatly reduce the opportunity for water quality degradation when integrated pest management systems are used. Agricultural chemicals that are properly used should be applied as needed by the plants to minimize the chances for leaching from rain storms or over irrigation. Planting and harvesting techniques should also consider the potential for water quality degradation. Field erosion can also transport pollutants such as sediment and phosphorous to surface waters and thus needs to be controlled.

1.12 Salinity management issues

Salinity management issues relate to the same water application conditions noted above. Water seepage at any facility or from an irrigated field within the system moves through the soil mass causing leaching of salts and other pollutants or elements that often collect at a point which is normally not desired by farmers or managers of the system. Salinity management also requires careful consideration of leaching fractions so excessive irrigation water is not applied to move salts not only out of the root zone but well beyond the field soil profile thus mobilizing excess salts and other pollutants needlessly. Within a scheme full consideration should be given to the reuse of drainage water if water balance and water quality de terminations do not require discharges of a predetermined quantity and quality to downstream users.

1.13 Leaching requirements

According to ASCE (1990), "the amount of leaching needed to maintain a viable irrigated agriculture depends on the salt content of the irrigation water, soil, and ground water; the salt tolerance of the crop; the climate; and the soil and water management". ASCE goes on to state that "the only economical way to control soil salinity is to ensure a net downward flow of water through the root zone to a suitable disposal site. If leaching is inadequate, harmful amounts of salt can accumulate within a few cropping seasons". This same source goes on to discuss formulas for determining proper leaching and details for proper control of salinity in the crop root zone. Water quality functions within the scheme and throughout the region can be directly impacted by not controlling the leaching excesses or over irrigating.

1.14 Within scheme reuse of drain water

Water is a precious commodity, and drain water can often be reused within the scheme area for productive purposes. Depending on the extent of degradation by the initial irrigation, reuse of less sensitive crops, trees or grasses is often possible. Downstream rights to water quantity and quality must be considered in planning these in-scheme reuse systems to assure that legal considerations are met. Sometimes environmental values can be improved by reusing the drainage water do· develop wetlands or windbreaks. Wetlands will be discussed later but can even provide the benefit of reducing some of the pollutants as the drain water passes through a series of these vegetative filter areas to the point of discharge back to the outlet for the scheme or project. Windbreaks often are needed adjacent to irrigated areas to provide control from desertification in arid climatic zones.

1.15 Water table management

Water table management involves controlling the drainage water levels to provide a sub-irrigation from the capillary rise. In some cases, full sub-irrigation can be introduced by adding water to the drainage system in dry periods to maintain a water table that will provide the crop water requirements. The practice is not thoroughly evaluated for arid and semi-arid regions where complications due to the control of salinity make management difficult and risks of salinization high. Some of the Mediterranean Region should be quite adaptable to good water table management systems. The system is particularly adaptable to flat humid lands where drain outlets can be modified to control the depth of water in a drain. Madramootoo (1996) indicated this practice has enormous potential for reducing nitrate pollution in subsurface drainage effluent in flat, humid regions. An elevated water table enhances denitrification, thereby reducing nitrate concentrations in the drain discharge (Gilliam and Skaggs, 1986). In the humid region of eastern Canada, Kaluli and Madramootoo (995) showed that by keeping the water table at 50 to 75 cm from the soil surface, nitrate losses can be reduced by 58 percent, compared to a free outlet, conventional drainage under intensively cropped grain corn.

1.16 Management and disposal of drainage water

Water quality from irrigated areas varies significantly in accordance with the crops grown, the efficiency of the irrigation and drainage systems, the pollutants introduced by urban and village populations, the quality of water discharged from industries within the scheme area, and the reuse that is made of waters within the system. Often it is beneficial to reuse the drain water that is to be discharged for environmental improvement or mitigation. It is sometimes possible to also use the project effluent for growing salt tolerant vegetation that has an economic value. Biological and chemical treatments may be required under some conditions to protect downstream interests. Wetland developments, stabilization ponds and evaporation ponds are also used under some conditions. In line with the rights of downstream users, it may even be necessary to provide dilution of the system wastewater to meet requirements agreed upon in treaties or protocols. The easiest disposal is direct discharge to the ultimate disposal point of most river systems, the sea.

1.17 Using saline drainage water

Saline drainage water can often be used to enhance or mitigate environmental values downstream from or adjacent to irrigation areas. These saline discharges can also be used in many cases to grow salt tolerant plants. Water quality, particularly the salinity content of the discharged waters, play a big part in the applicability of these practices. The acceptable parameters are so variable that field pilot installations are normally required to test the proposals that seem the most viable.

1.18 Environmental uses

Environment values are a key concern for irrigation project management and drainage water can provide help in minimizing these problems. Saline drainage water must be treated as a resource and used to enhance or mitigate environmental values under many situations. In desert environments windbreaks are critical to the protection of irrigated agricultural systems. The planned development of windbreaks using very salt tolerant trees has been used in China's Tarim River Basin for many years. It is also possible to develop or improve wetland areas near projects with the drainage water. Constructed wetlands and natural wetlands can even be managed to improve the water quality to some degree.

1.19 Using saline water for growing salt tolerant plants

The production of salt tolerant vegetation using drainage water is practical for many locations. In these systems the drain water is continually reused to irrigate salt tolerant crops, trees, and halophytes. The fmal effluent is disposed of in a solar evaporator so downstream water quality is not degraded. Madramootoo (1996) reported that in California for one pilot project, the final drainage volume was reduced by about one-tenth, and its salt and selenium concentrations increased 10 and 2 fold, respectively. For a cropland are of 1,000 ha, the area of salt tolerant trees is 20 ha, and the halophytes cover 8 ha, and the area of the solar evaporator is 4 ha. Materials in the solar evaporator may have a marketable value and the production of crops, trees and grass for biomass certainly has some value

1.20 Biological and chemical treatments

Advances in recent years in the biological and chemical treatment of drainage water have been made. FAO and ICID (1997) have prepared a document that is being printed titled, "Management Guidelines for Agricultural Drainage and Water Quality". A chapter within this document deals with drainage water treatment and discusses the selection of a treatment process and provides a brief discussion about the multitude of treatment methods and processes.

1.21 Constructed wetlands, stabilization ponds and evaporation ponds

Constructed wetlands can also be used to improve water quality from disposal drains. Ochs *et al.* (1996) notes that flow through wetlands have promise for providing improved discharges from irrigation projects by constructing them in series with varying types of vegetation. Filtration potential for sediments help control those pollutants that attach to soil particles and vegetative uptake by plants help remove some pollutants that move with the water flow. Treatment of drain effluents in stabilization ponds is commonly used for domestic wastewater management. FAO and ICID (1997) provides guidance for these systems as well as evaporation ponds. Applicability of each type of system requires careful study. Water quality can be improved with stabilization ponds, but evaporation ponds concentrate salts and other elements and dangers of developing toxic levels of elements such as selenium must be carefully evaluated.

1.22 Dilution

Dilution of the drainage water from an irrigated area is sometimes necessary to meet downstream water quality standards or treaties. This requires valuable water that could be used for irrigation or another beneficial use in the irrigated area and provides an extra incentive to minimize degradation of the water quality within the irrigation scheme.

1.23 Discharge

The ultimate disposal is normally to the sea and discharge of the poorer quality water can also degrade estuary ecosystems. Care must be take in selecting discharge points to minimize environmental problems from drain discharges. It is important to monitor the water quality from these discharges to watch for significant changes in the drainage effluent that could lead to environmental problems. If changes are noted, steps should be taken to alleviate the problem condition that has developed in the irrigation area or other contributing watershed.

1.24 Monitoring and evaluation

Water quality control is critical to the success of any irrigation project. The quality of water is a dynamic value with many components and requires careful monitoring and evaluation to manage the system for water quality protection. Monitoring must be systematic, continuous and include measurements related to the water source, within the scheme and the outlet. Irrigated areas should support river basin management systems that they are a part of. The integrated monitoring of all organizations concerned with water quality in a basin should be the goal of all irrigation scheme management authorities.

1.25 Conclusion

Salt-affected soils develop from a wide range of factors including: soil type, field slope and drainage, irrigation system type and management, fertilizer and manuring practices, and other soil and water management practices. In Colorado, perhaps the most critical factor in predicting, managing, and reducing salt-affected soils is the quality of irrigation water being used. Besides affecting crop yield and soil physical conditions, irrigation water quality can affect fertility needs, irrigation system performance and longevity, and how the water can be applied. Therefore, knowledge of irrigation water quality is critical to understanding what management changes are necessary for longterm productivity.

References

Ayers RS, Westcot DW. 1985. Water quality for agriculture. FAO irrigation and drainage paper 29 rev 1. Food and agriculture organization of the United Nations, Rome, Italy, 174 pp.

Balba AM. 1995. Management of problem soils in arid ecosystems. CRC/Lewis Publishers, Boca Raton, 250 pp.

Bauder TA, Waskom RM, Sutherland PL, Davis JG. 2011. Irrigation water quality criteria. Colorado State University Extension Publication, Crop series/irrigation. Fact sheet no. 0.506, 4 pp.

Bresler E, McNeal BL, Carter DL. 1982. Saline and sodic soils. Principles-dynamics-modeling. Advanced Series in Agricultural Sciences 10. Springer-Verlag, Berlin/Heidelberg/New York, 236 pp.

Eaton FM. 1950. Significance of carbonates in irrigation waters. Soil Sci 69:123–133

FAO/UNESCO. 1973. Irrigation, drainage and salinity. An International source book. Unesco/ FAO, Hutchinson & Co (Publishers) Ltd, London, 510 pp.

Follett RH, Soltanpour PN. 2002. Irrigation water quality criteria. Colorado State University Publication No. 0.506 Kinje JW (1993) Environmentally sound water management: Irrigation and the environment. Proceedings of the International Symposium on Environmental Assessment and Management of Irrigation and Drainage Projects for Sustained Agricultural Growth, 24–28 October 1993, Lahore, Pakistan, pp 14–44.

GA. 1960. Tolerance of crops to exchangeable sodium. USDA Information Bulletin No 216, 4 pp Shahid SA. 2004. Irrigation water quality manual. ERWDA Soils Bulletin No 2, 29 pp.

Ludwick AE, Campbell KB, Johnson RD, McClain LJ, Millaway RM, Purcell SL, Phillips IL, Rush DW, Waters JA. 1990. Water and plant growth. In: Western Fertilizer Handbook – horticulture Edition, Interstate Publishers Inc, Illinois, pp 15–43.

Maas EV. 1987. Salt tolerance of plants. In: Christie BR (ed) Handbook of plant science in agriculture. CRC Press, Boca Raton, pp 57–75.

Shahid SA, Mahmoudi H. 2014. National strategy to improve plant and animal production in the United Arab Emirates. Soil and water resources Annexes.

USSL Staff. 1954. Diagnosis and improvement of saline and alkali soils. USDA Handbook No 60. Washington DC, USA 160 pp.

Wilcox LV, Blair GY, Bower CA. 1954. Effect of bicarbonate on suitability of water for irrigation. Soil Sci 77:259–266.

Wilcox LV. 1960. Boron injury to plants. USDA Bulletin No 211, 7 pp.

2

Drip Irrigation Systems One Drop is Life

2.1 Introduction

Water is the most precious gift of the nature and it is also the most crucial element for sustainability of the life in the earth. India is the largest user of freshwater in the world. India's total water consumption alone is the higher than any other continents. The Agricultural sector is the largest consumer of water followed by the domestic sector and the industrial sector. The role of irrigation water as one of the most essential inputs for crop cultivation can't be denied. As a traditional productive input, it ensures production by acting as an agent of insurance against inadequate and inconsistent monsoon. Ultimately the outcome provides agricultural production stability. Thus, irrigation is of prime importance in cultivation of vegetable crops as it ensures favourable water balance within the root zone in addition to natural precipitation. It fulfils the crop- water demand and improves the crop production and effectiveness of other agricultural inputs. It is also an important limiting factor of crop yield, because of its association with several factors of plant environment, which directly influence the crop growth and development (Yaghi *et al.*, 2013). The various irrigation methods under different system of irrigation differ with regard to extent of control, timeliness and adequacy of supply of irrigation water for crop cultivation. Consequently, the economic benefits and the costs due to these irrigation methods vary among different irrigation systems. The dominant method of irrigation practiced in large parts of the country is surface irrigation (basin, border and furrow) where the entire soil surface is almost flooded without considering the actual consumptive requirements of the crops. Frequent over or under irrigation create the problems of water stress or water logging leading to reduced irrigation efficiency (less than 30%). Thus, in this method crop utilize only less than one half of the water released and remaining half gets lost in conveyance, application, runoff and evaporation. Therefore, to make the best use of water for agriculture and to improve water productivity is a pre requisite. This highlights the need to adopt modern efficient irrigation method. Micro irrigation (MI) methods like drip and sprinklers need to be employed for efficient distribution and application of water for crop production. Drip and sprinkler irrigation is a solution that reduces conveyance and distribution losses and allows higher water use efficiency. Drip irrigation has been found very effective in vegetable production. Efficient use of available water in vegetable production can be achieved by adopting water management practices and adoption of drip irrigation technology is one of them.

2.2 Drip Irrigation

Drip irrigation system is extremely profitable as it saves 40-70 percent water and enhanced the water use efficiency by 90-95 percent as compared to surface irrigation method, i.e., flood, sprinkler, furrow. It also reduces labour cost, protects the plants from diseases by minimizing humidity in atmosphere and ultimately increases the productivity. Beside this, water soluble fertilizers can also be applied through irrigation water. Thus, drip irrigation has become a means of Hi-tech Agriculture/Horticulture and precision farming.

Drip irrigation is an effective irrigation system that permits application of water to plants to closely meet the consumptive use requirements. Drip irrigation is a technique in which water is applied in small and precise amount at frequent intervals, directly near the root zone, through emitting devices via a network of PVC/HDPE mains, sub mains, filtration unit, control valves and LLDPE laterals. It minimizes the wastage of water by delivering the water very near to root zone. In this system water is applied to each plant separately in small, frequent, precise quantities through dripper emitters. It is the most advantage irrigation method with the highest application efficiency. The water is delivered continuously in drops at the same point and moves into the soil and wets the root zone vertically by gravity and laterally by capillary action. The planted area is only partially wetted. In medium-heavy soils of good structure, the lateral movement of the water beneath the surface is greater than in sandy soils. Moreover, when the discharge rate of the dripper exceeds the soil intake rate and hydraulic conductivity the water becomes pond on the surface. This results in the moisture being distributed more laterally rather than vertically. The following table indicates the water lateral spread values.

The drippers are small-sized emitters made up of high-quality plastics. They are mounted on small soft pipes at frequent spaces. Water enters the dripper emitters at approximately 1.0 bar and is delivered at zero pressure in the form of continuous droplets at low rates of 1.0 -0.24 litres per hour. Drippers are connected to the laterals either on-line, i.e, inserted in the pipe wall by the aid of a punch; or in-line, where the pipe is cut to insert the dripper manually or with a machine.

Drip irrigation is mainly applied in intensive cultivations planted in rows like vegetables, fruit trees, melons, bananas, papayas, grapes, etc. This technology has the greatest potential where water is either very expensive or scarce or the soils are coarse textured. In drip irrigation the drippers and/or the lateral spacing are directly related to the crop planting spacing. In most vegetable crops, the dripper spacing is identical to the crop planting spacing, i.e., one dripper per plant and one dripper lateral per row of cultivation. With drip tapes there are several emission points per plant in order to ensure a continuous wetted strip along the row. Here the arrangement is one drip tape per row of crop. Under drip irrigation most of the vegetable develop the bulk of their roots in the first 30 cm depth of the soil profile below the emission point. Thus if both the crop and the emission points along the rows are closely spaced, most of the soil volume can be sufficiently wetted with optimum results. Where the crop is planted closely in beds, one dripper lateral per two rows can be applied with good results. Celery, capsicum and hot peppers planted in double rows are also irrigated by one dripper lateral placed in between the rows. The technology assumes a special significance in Himalayan regions, which are endowed with undulating topography, are difficult to level and having higher runoff rates. Micro-irrigation was practiced in India through indigenous methods such as bamboo pipes, perforated clay pipes and pitcher/porous cup irrigation. Drip-irrigation also enables the use of fertilizers, pesticides and other soluble chemicals along with the irrigation water more economically.

2.3 History

Drip irrigation was used in ancient times by filling buried clay pots with water and allowing the water to gradually seep into the soil. Modern drip irrigation began its development in Germany in 1860 when researchers began experimenting with subsurface irrigation using clay pipe to create combination irrigation and drainage systems. In 1913, E.B. House at Colorado State University succeeded in applying water to the root zone of plants without raising the water table. Perforated pipe was introduced in Germany in the 1920s. In 1934, O.E. Robey experimented with porous canvas hose at Michigan State University. With the advent of modern plastics during and after World War II, major improvements in drip irrigation became possible. Plastic micro-tubing and various types of emitters began to be used in the greenhouses of Europe and the United States.

A new technology of drip irrigation was then introduced in Israel by Simcha Blass and his son Yeshayahu. Instead of releasing water through tiny holes (blocked easily by tiny particles), water was released through larger and longer passageways by using friction to slow water inside a plastic emitter. The first experimental system of this type was established in 1959 in Israel by Blass, where he developed and patented the first practical surface drip irrigation emitter. In 1973, publisher Massada Limited in Israel printed a book in Hebrew by Simcha Blass named "WATER IN STRIFE AND ACTION." Blass was a well-known water engineer in Israel in its first years and chief engineer in Jewish Yishuv. He planned the Israeli main water carrier. It is a common misconception that drip irrigation was invented in Israel. There is no question that much of the product innovation in this field occurred in Israel and that companies in Israel have contributed significantly to the industry, but they cannot take all the credit for its development. The facts are that drip irrigation system, with plastic pipes and the new plastic drippers, was invented and first used and developed in Israel by Blass. It does not change the contributions made earlier and later.

This method subsequently spread to Australia, North America, and South America by the late 1960s. In the United States, in the early 1960s, the first drip tape, called Dew Hose, was developed by Richard Chapin of Chapin Watermatics. In 1969, researchers under Prof. R. K. Sivanappan at Tamil Nadu Agricultural University in Coimbatore, India started research using drip irrigation using the available tubes and micro tubes in the market not only in the research station, but also in the farmer's field for banana, grapes, cotton, and vegetables. Beginning in 1987–88, Jain irrigation toiled and struggled to pioneer water-management through drip irrigation with the advice of Dr. Sivanappan. Jain irrigation (www.jains.com) also introduced some hi-tech drip irrigation concepts to Indian agriculture such as "Integrated System Approach," One-Stop-Shop for Farmers, "Infrastructure Status to Drip Irrigation & Farm as Industry." They have established "Research and Demonstration Farm" for modern drip irrigation concepts at Hi-tech Agricultural Institute near Jalgaon–Maharashtra–India. Jains opened a head office in Fresno–CA. The area under drip irrigation is more than five lakh hectares covering about 30 crops including grapes, sugarcane, banana, cotton, horticultural crops, vegetables, and fruits.

The first drip irrigation system in Puerto Rico was installed in 1970 for fruit orchard owned by Luciano Fuentes in Coamo municipality, and in mango orchard at Fortuna Agricultural Experimental Substation in Juana Diaz municipality. In 1979, first experiment on drip irrigation was established at Fortuna Substation by Megh R. Goyal, Father of Irrigation Engineering in Puerto Rico. Today, acreage under drip irrigation for vegetables and fruits has increased to more than 60,000 acres in Puerto Rico.

It is assumed that the drip irrigation will fortify agriculture and increase efficiency of food production. With this system, the plant can efficiently use available natural resources such as: soil, water, and air. The drip irrigation is also known as "daily irrigation," "trickle irrigation," "daily flow irrigation," or "micro irrigation," The term "trickle" was originated in England, "drip" in Israel, "daily flow" in Australia and "micro irrigation" in USA. The difference is only in the name, and all these terms have the same meaning. The water in a drip irrigation system flows in three forms:

i) It flows continuously throughout the lateral line.
ii) It flows from an emitter or dripper connected to the lateral line.
iii) It flows through orifices perforated in the lateral line.

2.4 Advantages of drip irrigation

Well-designed drip irrigation system can increase the crop yield due to following factors:

A. Efficient use of the water:

- It reduces the direct losses by evaporation.
- It does not cause wetting of the leaves.
- It does not cause movement of drops of water due to the effect of wind.
- It reduces consumption of water by grass and weeds.
- It eliminates surface drainage.
- It allows watering the entire field until the edges.
- It allows applying the irrigation to an exact root depth of crops.
- It allows watering greater land area with a specific amount of water.

B. Reaction of the plant:

- It increases the yield per unit (hectare-centimetre) of applied water.
- It improves the quality of crop and fruit.
- It allows more uniform crop yield.

C. Environment of the root:

- It improves ventilation or aeration.
- It increases quantity of available nutrients.
- The conditions are favourable for retention of water at low tension.

D. Control of pests and diseases:

- It increases efficiency of sprayings of insecticides and pesticides.
- It reduces development of insects and diseases.

E. Correction of problem of soil salinity:

- The increase in salts happens at a distance away from the plant.

- It reduces salinity problems. A greater reduction is obtained by increasing the water flow. Salts are limited to an outer periphery of a wetted zone.

F. Weed control:

- It reduces the growth of weeds in the shaded humid space.

G. Agronomic practices:

- The activities of the irrigation do not interfere with those of the crop, the plant protection, and the harvesting.
- It reduces inter cultivation, since there is less growth of weeds.
- Helps to control the erosion.
- It reduces soil compaction.
- It allows applying fertilizers through the irrigation water—called fertigation.
- It increases work efficiency in fruit orchards, because the space between the rows is maintained dry.

H. Economic benefits:

- The cost is lower compared with overhead sprinkler and other permanent irrigation systems.
- The cost of operation and maintenance is low. The costs are high when the average row spacing is less than three meters.
- It can be used in uneven terrains.
- The water application efficiency is high. Energy use per acre is reduced due to smaller diameter pipes, and only 50-60% of water is used.
- The BC ratio is favourable and the payback period is one to two years.

2.5 Disadvantages of drip irrigation

A. The drip irrigation, like other methods of irrigation, cannot adjust to all the specific crops, sites, and objectives

B. The system has the following problems and limitations:

- The drippers are obstructed (or clogged) easily with soil particles, algae or mineral salts.
- The soil moisture is limited. The soil moisture volume depends on the discharge of drippers, dripper spacing, and the soil type.
- The rodents or insects can damage some components of the drip irrigation system.
- A more careful high technology management is needed compared to other irrigation systems.

- The initial investment and annual cost are higher compared to other irrigation methods.
- It requires high initial investment.
- Frequent clogging of drippers. The clogging could be due to algae, salt accumulation or foreign particles and insufficient filtration of impurities in the irrigation water.
- Non availability of technical manpower.
- Inadequacy of technical input for efficient management of drip irrigation system.
- It is not suited for frost protection or for cooling during periods of hot weather.
- They are not suited for supplemented irrigation of large areas.
- Availability of components and cost of spares.

2.6 Suitability of Drip Irrigation

2.6.1 Crops

Drip irrigation is most suitable for vegetables, fruits, sugarcane, and cereal crops except paddy. The high value crops such as fruit crops give early recovery of capital investment on installation of a micro irrigation system. These systems are also suitable for plantation crops such as coconut, coffee, cardamom, cumin, citrus, grapes and mango. Close growing crops will require more investment, otherwise for widely spaced crops, these systems can be easily installed.

2.6.2 Slopes

Drip irrigation is adaptable to any cultivable slope. Normally the crops and laterals are planted along contour lines. This practice minimizes the change in emitter discharge due to change in land elevations.

2.6.3 Soils

Drip irrigation is suitable for most of the soils. For example, on clay soils, irrigation water should be applied slowly to avoid ponding and runoff. On sandy soils, higher emitter discharge will be appropriate to ensure lateral movement of the water into the soil. It can be applied to irrigate crops grown on undulating land topography and slopes where the depth of soil is limited.

2.6.4 Irrigation Water

One of the major problems with drip irrigation is emitters clogging. All emitters have very small openings ranging from 0.2-2.0 mm in diameter and these can be clogged with the use of dirty water. Thus, it is essential to install filters for irrigation water to be free from sediments. Micro sprinklers can eliminate problem of clogging to a certain extent. Clogging may also occur if the water contains algae, fertilizer deposits and dissolved chemicals which precipitate such as calcium and iron. Filtration may remove some of the materials. Drip irrigation is also suitable for poor quality water (saline water). Supplying water to individual plants also means that the method can be efficient to increase the water use efficiency and thus most suitable where water is scarce resources.

2.6.5 Wetting Patterns

Due to the manner in which water is applied by a drip irrigation system, only a portion of the soil surface and root zone of the total field is wetted unlike surface and sprinkler irrigation systems. Water flowing from the emitter is distributed in the soil by gravity and capillary forces creating the contour lines similar to onion shape. The exact shape of the wetted volume and moisture distribution will depend on the soil texture, initial soil moisture, and to some degree, on the rate of water application. The water savings that can be made using drip irrigation are the reductions in deep percolation, surface runoff and evaporation from the soil. Soil moisture content in the soil always remains at or around the field capacity in drip irrigation, where as in sprinkler and surface irrigation methods, crops face over irrigation and water stress during certain period. In the line source type of drip irrigation system where the emitters are spaced very closely, individual onion patterns creates a continuous moisture zone. The knowledge about the wetting patterns under emitters is essential in selecting the appropriate spacing of the emitters. Distance between emitters and emitter flow rates must match to the wetting characteristics of the soil and the amount and timing of water to be supplied to meet the crop needs.

Under drip irrigation, the ponding zone that develops around the emitter is strongly related to both the application rate and the soil properties. The water application rate is one of the factors which determine the soil moisture regime around the emitter and the related root distribution and plant water uptake patterns. Drip irrigation systems generally consist of emitters that have discharge varying from 2.0 to 8.0 lph. In semi-arid climates, crop water use during the summer can be 6 to 8 mm/d with water supplied two or three times a week. When the water application exactly equal to the plant water need, then also, part of the water may not be used by the plant and it would most likely leach below the root zone. Therefore, lowering the emitter discharge to as close as possible to the plant water uptake rate can improve irrigation efficiency. Recently, micro drip irrigation systems have been developed that provide emitter discharges of 0.5 lph. These systems have been studied most intensively in greenhouses (Koenig, 1997), and preliminary results showed that they reduced water consumption of tomato plant by 38%, increased yield by 14 to 26%, and reduced leaching fraction by 10 to 40%. In a recent application on sweet corn under field conditions, Assouline *et al.* (2002) have shown that micro drip irrigation may improve yield, reduce drainage flux, and affect the water content distribution within the root zone, especially through an increased drying of the 0.60 to 0.90m soil layer compared with conventional drip irrigation.

The micro drip technology still raises some problems concerning the uniformity of application and the steadiness of the discharges. However, soil moisture regimes similar to those resulting from continual low water application rates can be achieved by means of pulsed drip irrigation. Infiltration experiments on a sandy loam soil showed that the water content distribution and the rate of wetting front advance under a pulsed water application were similar to water applied in a continuous manner, and those temporal fluctuations in flux and in soil water content exponentially damped with depth for periodic pulses applied at the soil surface. Consequently, pulsed irrigation using conventional drip emitters could be one way of creating the water regime observed with continual low application rates while bypassing technical problems associated to micro drip emitters. The relationships between water application rates, soil properties, and the resulting water distribution for conventional emitters (2.0 lph) are well documented. The wetting patterns during application generally consist of two zones: (i) a saturated zone close to the emitter, and (ii) a zone where the water content decreases toward the wetting front. Increasing the emission rate generally results in an increase in the wetted soil diameter and a decrease in the wetted depth (Schwartzman and Zur, 1986; Ah Koon *et al.*, 1990). In micro drip irrigation, field observations seem to indicate that there is no saturated zone and that the wetted soil volume is greater compared with that for conventional emitter discharges (Koenig, 1997). The relationship between the water application rate and the resulting water content distribution is complex because it is a three-dimensional outcome related to soil properties and crop uptake characteristics. Therefore, a quantitative representation of the flow processes by means of a simulation model could be beneficial in studying the effects of emitter discharge on the water regime of drip irrigated crops.

2.7 Water Requirement through Drip Irrigation

With regard to vegetable crops, generally, yield decreases significantly in the absence of sufficient water to fully replenish ET. In addition, the negative effects of limited irrigation water on the quality of vegetable crops further contribute to a substantial reduction of the marketable yield. Vegetable crops are sensitive to suboptimal irrigation with slight differences among cultivars.

The water requirement in drip irrigation system includes the crop demand to meet out losses due to evapotranspiration (ET) or consumptive use (Cu) and the quantity of water required for special operations such as leaching. Water requirement of crops under drip irrigation varies depending on the factors like

a) Type of the crop
b) Age of the crop
c) Effective root zone of the crop which varies according to growth stage
d) Season of the year
e) Evapotranspiration demand
f) Soil type

There is a close relationship between the rate of consumptive use by crops (ET) and the rate of evaporation from a well-located standard Evaporation Pan. The water requirement of different crops under drip irrigation system is generally estimated on daily basis by using the following equation as suggested by Shukla *et al.* (2001).

WR= Ep. Kp. Kc. Sp. Sr. Wp

Where, WR = Volume of water required (litre / day / plant)

Ep = Pan evaporation as measured by Class-A pan evaporimeter (mm /day)

Kc = Crop co-efficient (co-efficient depends on crop growth stage)

Kp = Pan co-efficient Sp = Plant to plant spacing (m)

Sr = Row to row spacing (m)

Wp = Fractional wetted area, which varies with different growth stage (0.3 to 1.0)

The water requirement thus determined to be fed to the root zone through the emitters. Depending upon the peak water requirement and time of irrigation, emitters are selected for discharge of 2lph, 3lph, 4lph etc. Lateral movement of water in the soil and the necessary wetted area to create the desired root system are directly related. The wetted area depends on soil characteristics specially infiltration capacity and lateral movement of the moisture in the soil, and on emitter discharge.

2.8 Components of Drip Irrigation Systems

A drip irrigation system consists of the components such as pump unit, fertigation equipment, filters, main, sub-main, laterals, and distributary outlets (emitters, micro-sprinklers, bubblers, etc.). Here we are concerned about drip system so we will talk about emitters in the following discussion. Besides, gate valves, check valves, pressure gauges and flow control valves are also used to regulate the flow of water and serve as additional components. The components of drip irrigation system can be grouped into two major heads as

i) Control head and

ii) Distribution network

2.8.1 Control Head

The control head of drip irrigation system includes the pump or overhead tank, fertigation equipment, filters, and pressure regulator.

2.8.2 Pump/Overhead Tank

It is required to provide sufficient pressure in the drip irrigation system. Centrifugal pumps are generally used for low pressure drip irrigation systems. Overhead tank is generally used for small areas of orchard crops with a comparatively less water requirement. The drip irrigation system requires energy to move water through the distribution pipe network and discharge it through emitters. In most irrigation systems, energy is imparted to water by a pump that in turn receives its energy from either an electric motor or an internal combustion engine. Therefore, it is important that both the pump and the engine be well suited to satisfy the requirements of the irrigation system. Usually, centrifugal pumps are used for this purpose. The characteristic curves of the pump are considered in selection of pumps. The characteristic curves show the relationship between capacity, head, power and efficiency of the pump. The head–capacity curve will give discharge of a pump at a given head. As the discharge increases, the head decreases. The pump efficiency increases with an increase in discharge but after a certain discharge, efficiency decreases. The BHP curve for a centrifugal pump increases over most of the range as the discharge increases. The pump horsepower at a maximum efficiency would be determined from the characteristic curves based on the irrigation system design discharge and the total dynamic head against which the pump is to operate. The total discharge and total dynamic head will be discussed later in this book. The following points should be considered for installation of a centrifugal pump.

The pump should be installed as close to the water source as possible.

- Foundations should be rigid enough to absorb all vibrations.
- The pump and driver must be aligned carefully.
- On the belt drive units, the pump and driver shaft must be parallel.
- The site selected should permit the use of minimum possible connections on suction and delivery pipes.

- Suction and delivery pipes should be supported independently of the pump.
- The suction pipe should be direct and short.
- The size of the suction pipe should be such that the velocity of water does not exceed 3 m/s.

2.8.3 Filtration System

The clogging of emitters is the main problem encountered in the operation of drip irrigation systems. Filtering and keeping contaminants out of the system are the main defence against the clogging caused by mineral and organic particles. Impurities in water can be classified into three categories:

- Inorganic solid particles: sand, silt and clay and insoluble precipitation.
- Living organisms such as algae, protozoa, bacteria, and fungi.
- Organic debris Removal of above-mentioned impurities is essential for efficient and trouble-free operation of a drip irrigation system which necessitates the use of proper filters.

2.8.3.1 Selection of Filters

While selecting filters for the drip irrigation system, the following factors are considered.

- The physical quality of water such as the concentration and pattern of the impurities, suspended solids and organic matter.
- The chemical nature of water such as pH level, and presence of sediments forming chemical elements and possible reaction with the injected fertilizers when fertigation is applied.
- Discharge and allowable head losses in the system. • Reliability and durability of the filters.
- Cost of the filter.
- The total surface area of the filtration element is very important. The filtration area needed for moderately dirt water is in the range of 60-150 cm^2 for drip irrigation.

2.8.3.2 Types of filters

Settling Basins: Settling basins can remove suspended material ranging from sand (2000 mm) to silt (200 mm) in stream water being used for irrigation. It removes large volumes of sand and silt. Basins are constructed so that it could limit turbulence and permit a minimum of 15 minutes of retention time for water to travel from the basin inlet to the pumping system intake. Longer retention time is required to allow the settling of smaller particles. A basin of

1.2 m deep, 3.3 m wide and 13.7 m long is required to provide a one quarter hour retention time for a 57 lps stream. Settling basin should be relatively long and narrow to eliminate short circuit current that reduces effective retention time. If the source of water is ground water, settling basins should not be used but if canal water is being used for irrigation through drip irrigation systems, it may be of a great use.

2.8.3.3 Media Filter

Media filters are used when irrigating with water containing high organic load such as water pumped from open water bodies or reclaimed water. It consists of fine gravel and sand of selected sizes placed in a pressurized tank. Media filters are not easily plugged by algae and can remove relatively large amounts of suspended solids before cleaning is needed. It can retain particle sizes in the range of 25 to 200 mm. In general water flow rates through the filters should be in between 10 to 18 lps per square meter of filtration surface area. Media filter should be followed by a secondary screen filter to prevent carryover of contaminants following the backwashing process. Numbers designate the sand media filter used in most drip irrigation filters: number 8 and 11 are crushed granite, and numbers 16, 20, and 30 are silica sands. The mean granule size in microns for each media number is approximately 1900, 1000, 825, 550 and 340 for number 8, 11, 16, 20, and 30, respectively.

2.8.3.4 Centrifugal Filter

The best treatment of the water containing soil particles is sedimentation of the particles by means of sand separators. Sand separators, hydro cyclones or centrifugal filters are synaminous which remove suspended particles that have specific gravity greater than 1.2. The centrifugal sand separator separates the sand and other heavy particles from the water by means of centrifugal force of the tangentially entering water into a conic tank (Fig. 3.6). The sand is thrown by the centrifugal force against the conic wall, settled down and accumulated in a collector at the bottom. The collector is washed out manually when full. The clean water is emitted in a spiral motion through an outlet at the top of the separator. The diameters of the top and bottom of the conical shape in centrifugal filter are designed in accordance with the flow of water. The centrifugal filters effectively remove large quantity of sand particles. They are placed often at the upstream of media or screen filters.

2.8.3.5 Screen Filter

Screen filters are fitted just after the pumping unit and no other filter is required if source of water is ground water. The casing is built of metal or plastic material. It has four apertures: water inlet, outlet, draining valve and cover.

It consists of a screen made of metal, plastic, or synthetic cloth enclosed in a special house used to limit maximum particle size. Screens are classified according to the number of openings per inch with standard wire size for each screen size. Most manufacturers recommend 100 to 200 mesh screens for drip irrigation system. Normally, the discharge through the screens is less than 135 lps per square meter of screen openings. A standard 200 mesh stainless steel screen has only 58% open area and equivalent nylon mesh with same size opening has only 24% open area. In screen filter, the mesh size and the total open area determine the efficiency and operational limits.

2.8.3.6 Disk Filters

This is more suitable for water with mixed impurities of inorganic solid particles and organic debris. The casing is made of metal or plastic material. The filtration element is made of stacked grooved ring-shaped disks, tightened together by a threaded cap. Water is filtered as it flows through the grooves. Coarse particles are trapped on the external surface of the stack while finer particles and organic debris adheres to the inner grooves. The discs are pressed together during filtration and direction of flow is reversed during back flushing mode. The discs start a spinning motion and complete retained impurities are removed. The discs are assembled in a cylinder and are pressed together. To handle large flow rate, they can be installed in batteries. The disk filters have much more higher dirt retention capacity than screen filters with the same specifications. Such filters are often used as final filtering component before the water enters the system.

2.8.4 Distribution Network

The distribution network constitutes main line, sub-main line and laterals with drippers and other accessories.

2.8.4.1 Main and Sub-main Line

A typical drip mainline is generally made of rigid Poly Vinyl Chloride (PVC) and High Density Polyethylene (HDPE). Pipes of 63 mm diameter and above with a pressure rating 4 to 6 kg/cm^2 are generally used for mainline pipes. The sub-main pipeline is made of rigid PVC, HDPE or LDPE (Low Density Polyethylene) of outside diameter ranging from 50 to 75mm with a pressure rating of 2.5 kg/cm^2. The diameters of main and sub-main pipelines are chosen based on estimated water to be carried out which ultimately needs the careful determination of peak crop water requirement. The sub-main line is connected to main line to deliver the water to laterals. Gate valve is provided on the sub-main line to control the flow and practiced when irrigating large area divided in many subplots. Each sub-plot will be irrigated with one sub-main. Sub-main line is fitted with a flushing valve to remove the contaminants. The main and sub-main lines are usually placed underground.

2.8.4.2 Laterals

Laterals are the pipes normally manufactured from LDPE or Linear Low Density Polyethylene (LLDPE). Generally, pipes having 12, 16 and 20 mm internal diameter with a wall thickness varying from 1 to 3mm are used as laterals. Nowadays even 32 mm lateral pipe is also being used. Since laterals are always laid over the surface, it must be flexible and non-corrosive. Pressure variation within the laterals lines must be within acceptable limits and therefore, selection of length and diameter of lateral line is a matter of accurate design.

2.8.4.3 Drippers/Emitters

The emitters are connected to the laterals and control the flow of water coming out of laterals. The design of single outlet emitter is based on the principle of energy losses by sudden change in velocity of fluid flow in the emitter path. The successive change in velocity occurs due to sudden enlargement and contraction in the designed flow path of the disc element. The necessary arrangement for expansion of flow is done by making larger cross-sectional area in the shape of circle and contraction of flow by smaller cross-sectional area in the shape of rectangular channel. The bottom of the path is made flat to increase the wetted perimeter of the flow passage, which leads to decrease the hydraulic radius and velocity of flow in the flow passage. The energy losses occur when the flow channel suddenly expands to a larger diameter circular path. The energy loss is accomplished by two ways – first due to the impulse momentum which takes place as the water flows from narrower rectangular passage to the wider circular passage and secondly when the water flows from wider circular section to the narrower channel section. In this process, a lot of eddies are formed which causes a considerable dissipation of energy. The high pressure from the lateral line transmitted into the emitter is greatly reduced and controlled flow of water emits in discrete drops almost at atmospheric pressure. Emitters are made from poly-propylene or polyethylene and available in the market in different types and designs. Point-source and line-source emitters operate either above or below the ground surface. Most of the point source emitters are either on-line or in-line emitters. The primary difference between on-line and in-line emitters is that the entire flow required downstream of the emitter passes through an in-line emitter. There is more head loss along a lateral with on-line emitters than one with in-line emitters because of obstruction created by the barbs of on-line emitters. The percentage area wetted, and the reliability of the emitters against the clogging and malfunctioning are two important aspects of quality and safety of drip irrigation systems. An ideal set of emitters should have the attributes such as durability, low cost, reliable performance with a relatively low rate of uniform discharge and relatively large and/or self-flushing passageway to reduce or prevent clogging.

2.8.4.4 Types of Drippers/Emitters

In-line Emitters: In-line emitters are fixed along with the lateral line. The pipe is cut and dripper is fixed in between the cut ends, such that it makes a continuous row after fixing the dripper. They have generally a simple thread type or labyrinth type flow path. (b) On-line Emitters: These are fixed on the lateral by punching suitable size holes in the pipe. These are of the following types:

i) Simple Type/Laminar Flow: In this type of dripper, the discharge is directly proportional to the pressure. They have simple thread type, labyrinth type, zig-zag path, vortex type flow path or have float type arrangement to dissipate energy.

ii) Turbo Key Drippers: These are made of virgin and stabilized polymers and are available in 2, 4 and 8 lph discharge. They provide resistance to blockage and are pressure compensating.

iii) Pressure Compensating Drippers: This type of dripper gives a fairly uniform discharge within the pressure range of 0.3 atmospheres to 3.5 atmospheres. They are provided with a high-quality rubber diaphragm to control pressure and are most suitable on slopes and difficult terrain.

iv) Built-in Dripper Tube: In this system, polyethylene drippers are inseparably welded to the inside of the tube during extrusion of polyethylene pipes. They are provided with independent pressure compensating water discharge mechanism and extremely wide water passage to prevent clogging. Other accessories include take out/ starter, rubber grommet, end plug, joints, tees and manifolds.

2.9 Some Review of Drip Irrigation in Vegetable Crops

2.9.1 Tomato

Sivanappan *et al.* (1998) reported that the yield of tomato under drip (8872 kg/ ha) was 43 percent higher as compared to furrow irrigation (6187 kg/ha) and the reduction in crop water requirement was to the tune of 78 percent. On silt clay loam soils of Bangladesh drip irrigation resulted in higher yields of tomato as compared to furrow method (Biswas *et al.* 2015). Increasing drip irrigation from 0.3Epan level to 0.7 Epan increased yield from 54 to 71 t/ha. However, the WUE was higher at 0.3 Epan irrigation (28 kg/ha-mm). The yield under drip (48 t/ha) was 50 percent more in comparison to flood-irrigated crop (32 t/ha). Irrigation water saving was to the tune of 31.5 percent with drip. Use of drip irrigation systems for tomato production in open as well as under mulch cultivation resulted in high fruit yields with good fruit size and cultivation resulted in high fruit yields with good fruit size.

2.9.2 Cabbage

Drip irrigation resulted in better growth and higher yields of cabbage with bigger head size of higher quality. The experimental findings of Singh *et al.* (1990) suggested that the trickle irrigation in heavy soils during winter season under shallow water table (1.8 to 2.2 m) conditions should be used with care. They obtained lower yields of cabbage crop under drip as compared to furrow irrigated crop, which was contrary to the general understanding that the crops under tickle irrigation perform better than the ones under surface irrigation.

2.9.3 Chillies

A study to find out the water requirement of chilli crop variety K-land and its response to drip irrigation was conducted at TNAU, Coimbatore in Tamil Nadu. There was saving of 62 per cent of water by drip irrigation. The yield of crop was increased by 25 per cent and reduced weed infestation by 50 per cent. Pandey *et al.* (2013) reported that the drip irrigation enhanced the fruit yicld, net income and minimized the time, weeds and diseases of the crop. Fertigation resulted in maximum yield (10.20 kg/m^2), minimal disease and saved water and total irrigation time as compared to top dressing. The drip irrigation had significantly increased yield (10.50 kg/m^2) and net income as compared to flood irrigation. Patel *et al.* (2017) took random sample of 12 chilli growers using drip irrigation system from 10 villages of Barwani district of Madhya Pradesh. Thus, total number of 120 chilli growers using drip irrigation system constituted the sample for the purpose of the study. This study reveals that 68.34 percent respondents had medium level of adoption regarding drip irrigation system, whereas, 100% respondents expressed the benefits of drip irrigation system as it increases the production and productivity of chilli and getting more income by the farmers. 91.66% respondents expressed the benefit of drip irrigation system for improving the socio-economic status of the farmers.

2.9.4 Capsicum

Paul *et al.* (2013) observed significantly higher fruit weight of capsicum under drip irrigation as compared to control practices. Capsicum yields with trickle irrigation were higher (74 t/ha) than those under sprinkler irrigation (59 t/ha) although similar soil moisture tensions were maintained under both the systems.

Capsicum gave higher yield with drip irrigation stystem as compared to furrow irrigation system and overall irrigation efficiencies were 37,65 and 84 per cent in furrow, sprinkler and drip irrigation, respectively Drip irrigation scheduled at 0.6 Epan gave higher yield (7.36 t/ha) than furrow irrigation scheduled at 0.6 Epan (6.08 t/ha) and 0.8 Epan (6.12 t/ha) level. Reducing irrigation application through drip by scheduling at 0.4 Epan during reproductive stage drastically reduced the yields. A comparison of drip and minisprinkler systems with surface method as control was studied both at Navsari and Pantnagar. While at both places the water savings with minisprinkler was almost same (19-20%) the water saving recorded ofr drip at Navsari was as low as 37 per cent as against 67% at Pantnagar. At both the places the yield increase was negligible. Contrarily in Maharashtra the yield increased ranging from 29 to 44 per cent. But the yield levels (3 to 6 t/ha) in two trials of Maharashtra were well below the yields achieved at Navsari and Pantnagar (11-12 t/ha). Further at Pune, for a yield level of 2.8 t/ha the water requirement through drip was 26 cm, at Rahuri it was 42 cm to achieve a yield level of 6 t/ha and at Navasri where the yield level was 11.8 t/ ha the water requirement was 70 cm.

2.9.5 Brinjal

According to Kumar *et al.* (2016) water use efficiency (yield per unit area per unit depth of water used) decreased with increase in irrigation levels for all the treatments of drip irrigation system. The increase in water use efficiency for drip irrigation system, Among the drip irrigation levels, the highest field water use efficiency (6148.31 kg/ha/cm) was found at 65% irrigation level, indicating comparatively more efficient use of irrigation water with a possibility of water saving of 35% water by adopting brinjal plot (1.58 litre/plant/day). An improvement in yield from 16 to 63 per cent and the saving in water to the tune of around 50 per cent were also reported from Patna (Annual Report, 2015-16). In Gujarat while the saving in water was around 25 percent. The yield increase was about 42 percent. A one-year trial conducted at Pantnagar showed that with mini sprinkler the yield was more than drip but water saving was less. The maximum water saving of 65 percent was recorded at Coimbatore, but at this level of water saving there was no improvement in the yield. At Pune the maximum improvement in yield (63%) was reported with simultaneous saving in irrigation water to the tune of 56 per cent.

2.9.6 Okra

In okra by adopting drip irrigation a saving of 84 percent of irrigation water was possible in cv. Pusa Sawani. The maximum water saving has been reported from Coimbatore (84%) followed by Gujarat (47%) and Hyderabad (22%). In one of the three trials at Maharashtra, the water saving was reported to be

41 percent with about 7 percent increase in yield. But when the saving in water got reduced to 27 percent the percent increase in yield rose to about 32. At Pantnagar, it was observed that the yield could be increased by about 36 percent with water saving of about 47 percent. It could be further increased to 57 percent with mulch in Andhra Pradesh conditions. The yield increase was observed to be 22 percent with 50 per cent water saving with drip alone and 52 percent 62 per cent respectively when drip was coupled with mulching also. Similarly in Kerala with water saving of 25 percent while drip alone could increase the yields by 52 percent with the use of mulch, the yield was more than doubled (Muhammed *et al.* 2015).

2.9.10 Cucumber and Ridge gourd

Cucumber demands high temperatures and soil moisture for satisfactory yield, and under unfavourable climatic conditions, several problems may occur, such as the reduction of female flowers, delay in fruit growth and mineral disorders. The results of the study conducted in Syria indicated that drip irrigation with transparent mulch excelled all other treatments at yield and water use efficiency (WUE), where its yield was 63.9 t/ha, and WUE was 0.262 t/ha/mm, while drip irrigation with black mulch produced 57.9 t/ha, with a WUE of 0.238 t/ha/mm. However, cucumber yield and WUE declined in the no mulch treatments of DI and SI to reach 44.1 t/ha with 0.153 t/ ha/mm and 37.7 t/ha with 0.056 t/ha/mm, respectively. The results showed that (DI + TM) treatment gave the highest soil temperature and moisture during both seasons in comparison to (DI + BM). This enhanced its vegetative growth and almost doubled its productivity compared to the SI treatment (Yaghi *et al.* 2013). As shown in Fig. 1 drip irrigated vegetable showed higher water productivity and required less water to produce per kg of cucumber and ridge gourd as compare to surface irrigated crop. Irrigation through drip saved 28.2% and 22% irrigation water as compare to surface irrigation in cucumber and ridge gourd, respectively (Annual Report 2015-16).

2.9.11 Potato, Cauliflower, French bean and Pea

Jha *et al.* 2017 conducted an experiment on evaluation of drip and furrow irrigation methods in participatory mode at the farmer's field of the eastern plateau and hill region. Comparative assessment in terms of yield gain, water productivity (WP) and net returns was carried out for tomato, potato, cauliflower, french bean and pea cultivated in the farmers' fields at Saraitoli village of Ranchi district of Jharkhand. The study revealed that, for the selected vegetables, adoption of drip irrigation improved the yields in the range of 38.2 to 65.8 % over furrow irrigation with highest yield increase in case of pea (65.8%) and tomato (58.7%) as shown in Table 2. Drip irrigation consistently recorded higher water productivity (WP) with more than five folds increase in case of potato and cauliflower.

2.10 Conclusion

Now the whole world is facing twin challenges of water stress and food insecurity that are growing continuously. The agricultural sector is the largest user of water and water is also a key resource for food production. So, neither of these two challenges can be defined in isolation. Producing more food for each drop of water will be a crucial strategy to address both challenges. Water productivity is an important driver in projecting future water demands. Efficient irrigation technologies like drip irrigation can help to establish greater control over water delivery (water control) to the crop roots, reduce the non-beneficial evaporation from field and non-recoverable percolation and return flows into 'sinks' and often increases the beneficial ET. Water productivity improves with the reduction in depleted fraction and yield enhancement. So, drip irrigation is the best method to improve yield as well as water productivity.

References

American Society of Civil Engineers, Committee on Irrigation Water Requirements of the Irrigation and Drainage Division of the ASCE. 1990. Evapotranspiration and Irrigation Water Requirements: a Manual. 332 p.

Badr, A.E., Ebabi, F.G., ELtomy, E.O. 2006. Fertigation methods effects on water and fertilizer uniformity in drip irrigation. Misr J. Ag. Eng., 23(1):122-136.

Karmeli, D., Keller, J. 1975. Trickle Irrigation Design. Glendora, California: Rain Bird Sprinkler Manufacturing Corp.

Penman, H.L. 1948. Natural evaporation from open water, bare soil and grass, Proc. R. Soc. Lond., 193:120-145.

Ram Nivas, Singh, D., Rao, V.U.M. 2002. Practical manual on evapotranspiration estimation,CCS Haryana Agricultural University, Hisar, India.

Singh, V.P., Xu, C.Y. 1997a. Evaluation and generalization of 13 equations for determining free water evaporation. Hydrological Processes 11:311-323.

Thornthwaite, C.W. and J.R. Mather, 1955. The Water Balance. Publications in Climatology, Drexel Institute of Technology, Centerton, New Jersey, VIII(1).

Thornthwaite, C.W., 1948. An approach toward a rational classification of Climate. Geograph. Rev. 38(1):55-94.

Thornthwaite, C.W., Holzman, B. 1939. The determination of land and water surfaces, Month. Weather Rev., 67:4-11.

Tiwari, K.N, Ajai Singh, P.K. Mal, A. Pandey. 2001. Effect of crop geometry on yield and economics of okra (Abelmoschus exculentus (L.) Moench.) under drip irrigation. Jl. of The Institution of Engineers, Division of Agricultural Engineering, India.

Zella, L., Kettab, A. 2002. Numerical methods of microirrigation lateral design. Biotechnol. Agron. Soc Environ. 6(4):231-235.

3

Sustainable Management of Groundwater

3.1 Introduction

Groundwater constitutes about 89% of the total fresh water resources in the planet. But in recent years, due to over exploitation of ground water and erratic nature of monsoon, there has been depletion of ground water across the world. Depletion of ground water has reached to the extent that it is virtually impossible to get the water table back. Even though there is a possibility of recharge of water from the other areas, the process is very slow and may take one year to replenish one meter. In view of this management of ground water has become one of the most significant issues in recent times. Added to it, there are also environmental problems such as aqua for mining, salt water intrusion, stream base flow reduction etc. For several reasons the efficient management of ground water resources through market mechanism has become difficult. Against this context the present article attempts to analyze the need for sustainable ground water management in India. The article also briefly discusses the concept of sustainable ground water management, factors affecting ground water availability, different approaches towards developing and using available ground water without adversely affecting the hydro-geological balance. Further, the paper highlights strategies for sustainable groundwater management, including development of aquifers, rainwater harvesting and artificial recharge methods. The article offers some relevant policy recommendations for sustainable groundwater management in India.

3.2 Significance of Groundwater Management

Sub-Surface water, or groundwater, is fresh water located in the pore space of soil and rocks. It has been estimated that out of about 790 billion cubic meter of water that seeps into the soil, about 430 billion cubic meter remains in the top soil layers, and produces soil moisture which is essential for growth of vegetation. The remaining 360 billion cubic meters percolates into the porous strata and represents the actual enrichment of underground water. Out of this the water that can be extracted economically is only about 255 cubic billion meters. Thus, sustainable groundwater management plays significant role in overall development of a country. Groundwater is the primary source of water for drinking and irrigation. It is a unique resource, widely available, providing security against droughts and yet closely linked to surface water resources and the hydrological cycle. Its reliable supply, uniform quality and temperature, relative turbidity and pollution free, minimal evaporation losses, and low cost of development are attributes making groundwater more attractive when compared to other sources. Yet, at the same time population and economic growth halved to ever more demands on the world's groundwater resources and in many countries, there are already significant impacts due to inadequately-regulated groundwater pumping and/or from pollution due to inadequate management. Especially in developing countries, these trends can lead to large socioeconomic costs, often for the poor. With rapid growth in population, urbanization, industrialization and competition for economic development, groundwater resource has become vulnerable to depletion and degradation. Management of this valuable resource is determined by its accessibility and utility in terms of quantity and quality. Due to imbalance between demand and availability, management approaches are facing various ethical dilemmas. For an effective, efficient and sustainable groundwater resources development and management, the planners and decision makers have future challenges to assess the inextricable logical linkages between water policies and ethical consideration. Ground water being a hidden resource is often developed without proper understanding of its occurrence in time and space. Thus ground water management on scientific lines is the key for sustainability of this vital resource.

3.3 Groundwater Management in India: Major Issues

Groundwater and its proper use assume great significance for a country like India. Unfortunately, there is no accurate survey of ground water resources but, according to the estimate of National Commission for Commission on Agriculture, India's groundwater resources would be about 300 million-hectare-meters or about 10 times the annual precipitation. The annual exploitable potential is put at 45 million-hectare-meters. With the introduction of the new agricultural strategy in the early 1960s, there was an increasing use of tube-wells. Though in 1960, only one per cent of the net irrigated land received tube-well irrigation, by 1988 about 27% of the net irrigated area got the benefit of tube-well irrigation. By 2001, demands for industrial water also raised about 151 billion liters per day. The government initiatives to popularize deep bore wells for getting more water has led to water tables to go down and. At the same time there was not much interest and initiative in favour of recharging the groundwater. Groundwater being a dynamic and replenishable resource has to be estimated primarily based on the component of annual recharge which could be subjected to development by means of suitable structures and which could be depend on the hydro-geological and climatic conditions.

In India, data on groundwater levels are not widely published or made available outside government organizations. Extraction and recharge estimates are also unreliable. As a result, discussions on ground water depletion are always based on unrealistic data. However, it is a fact that falling water tables and depletion of economically accessible ground water reserves have serious socio-economic consequences in an agrarian country like India. Competition between rural and urban users is increasing and leads to conflict over ground water usage. Falling water tables also increase division among communities. Poor farmers are forced to abandon irrigation as falling water tables limit access to those who can afford to deepen wells. Deep wells need more electricity and thus lead to increase in energy related economic cost also. More over depletion of water tables will pose a threat to food security. Assured irrigation is important for food production. As water tables decline, poor farmers find it difficult to meet the huge energy requirement for deepening wells which ultimately lead to decline in food production. Therefore, it is needless to point out there is an urgent need for conservation of this vital resource for the preservation of environmental security and sustainable agricultural development.

3.4 Strategies of Groundwater Management

Understanding the importance of groundwater resources and the growing demand for it makes it impertinent to search for effective strategies for managing the groundwater. For an effective supply side management, it is essential to have full knowledge of hydrogeological controls that govern the yield and behaviour of ground water levels under abstraction stress, the interaction of surface and ground water in respect of river base flow and changes in flow and recharge dates due to their exploitation. Groundwater management policies therefore will need to address a multitude of issues including

- Management of supplies to improve water availability in time and space
- Management of demands including efficiency of water use, sectoral interaction with economic activities etc.
- Balancing competing demands and preservation of the integrity of water dependent eco system.

In demand side management socio economic dimension plays an important role involving managing the users of water and land. Mere regulatory interventions like water rights and permits and economic tools of water pricing etc cannot be successful unless the different user groups are fully involved. For effective management of groundwater resources there is a need to create awareness among the different water user groups and workout area specific plans for sustainable development. Thus ground water management not only requires proper assessment of available resources and understanding of interconnection between surface and groundwater system, but also actions required for proper resource allocation and prevention of the adverse effects of uncontrolled development of ground water resources. Sustainable development and management of groundwater requires the following strategies:

3.4.1 Scientific Development of Groundwater

Scientific development of groundwater involves a proper understanding of the local groundwater availability, its behaviour and demand centric development with scientific planning. The need for scientific development of groundwater under different hydrogeological conditions involves the following elements:

3.4.1.1 Development of Deep aquifers

In many parts of the country deep aquifers are not fully utilized or developed which led to under-utilization of available groundwater resources. This under-utilization from deep aquifers in some of the states including Haryana, U.P and Punjab, has resulted in a near stagnant condition at depths and provided the necessary time factor for the deterioration in quality of ground water. It is evident that the deeper aquifers in alluvial areas are not fully developed in upper reaches and the unutilized groundwater in confined aquifers ultimately is lost to the saline aquifers adjacent to the basin boundary. This development of deep aquifers is important for development and management of groundwater for sustainable use.

3.4.1.2 Development of groundwater in non- developed areas

Policy makers often pay attention to the regions where groundwater development has great potential and neglect other areas with hidden potential. In India, the eastern and northeastern region is yet to develop groundwater properly. Naturally, small farmers find it difficult to increase agricultural production due to non-availability of water. There is wide scope for development of groundwater in these areas which often faces floods during rainy seasons.

3.4.1.3 Development of Flood plain aquifers

Flood plains are good reservoirs of ground water. Thus, sustainable management of flood plain aquifers offers excellent scope for its development and additional requirement of water. The development of groundwater in Yamuna flood plain

Area in Delhi is an example of scientific management of water resources. Over development of shallow aquifers in flood plains creates the necessary sub-surface space for augmentation of groundwater from the river flows during the monsoon. Induced management is an effective management tool to meet the gap of demand and supply in areas adjacent to rivers with active flood plains. Thus proper development of flood plain aquifer is impertinent for groundwater development and management.

3.4.1.4 Development of groundwater in Water logged areas

The water-logged areas in canals command offer scope for ground water development by lowering the water table up to 6 meters or more. The inferior quality of water can be mixed with canal water in a proportion acceptable for irrigation. Thus additional water for irrigation can be created and more over the lower water table will help in rainfall recharge in the area that will help in improvement of soil and water quality.

3.4.1.5 Development of groundwater in Canal Commands

One of the effective strategies for sustainable ground water management is to use surface water in one area and utilize the recharge by development of groundwater in areas adjacent to canal commands. This would result not only in proper utilization of available water resources but also the pumpage from groundwater storage will provide a sub-surface drainage to the areas, which are likely to be water logged.

Apart from these development of groundwater in coastal areas also needs to be addressed for the proper utilization of water resources.

3.4.2 Artificial Recharge of groundwater

Another effective strategy is augmentation of available groundwater resources through rain water harvesting and artificial recharge. It is estimated that annually about 36.4BCM of surplus surface runoff can be recharged to augment the ground water. In rural areas, techniques of artificial recharge by modification of natural movement of water through suitable civil structures like Percolation tanks, Check dams, Nala Bunds, Gully Plugs etc. have been found feasible. The roof top rainwater harvesting structure is also feasible both by augmenting the groundwater storage as well as by storing it in specially built tanks.

3.4.3 Regulation of groundwater development

One of the important strategies for sustainable management of groundwater is regulation of groundwater development in critical areas. Over development of groundwater resources is increasingly being recognized as a major problem. The tendency towards over development of groundwater resources is rooted in the rapid spread of energized pumping technologies, resource characteristics, demographic shifts and government policies. There is very little efforts to check the over exploitation and regulation of ground water resource. At present the only actual management is by limiting NABARD funds in blocks classified as grey and dark. Gujarat has passed a ground water management Act for regulating and controlling use of groundwater. However, it is not easy to implement the legislations without people's support and awareness creation.

3.4.4 Ensuring water for agriculture

The major challenge is proper prioritization of water resource allocation without affecting the water tables and agricultural productivity. Thus any sustainable strategy should rely on the assessment of the actual water to be allotted for domestic use, agriculture and maintaining eco system balance. More specifically, it should focus on a cost effective analysis of using water for different use, adept and improver water productivity, irrigation efficiency and post-harvest processing. Some of the effective approaches, which can be applicable in India, include:

1. Encourage the non-sensitive ground water users to switch from exploitation of high quality aquifer to bad quality groundwater for major groundwater use.
2. Restrict withdrawal of abstraction rights from industries that have not installed water-efficient technologies.
3. Provide subsidies for improving the efficiency of irrigation water use in periurban areas in exchange for groundwater abstraction rights.

3.4.5 Checking Contamination of groundwater

There is urgent need to check the contamination level of groundwater the groundwater protection from pollution can be ensured by several ways including:

1. Preparing vulnerability maps, based on distribution of travel times, chemical parameters, types of topsoil, sub soil and land use.
2. Delineating and prioritizing areas of high groundwater vulnerability for main sewerage extension.
3. Locating of landfill facilities to areas of low ground water vulnerability
4. Restricting residential development served by inciting sanitation
5. Restricting the disposal of industrial discharges to the ground in vulnerable areas through introduction of discharge permits and appropriate charging to encourage recycling and reduction.

3.5 Limitations of Existing Approaches

Though there are existing of various strategies for sustainable management of groundwater resources, it often fails to create any positive impact on the sustainable use due to number of reasons. Due to absence of any pricing mechanism and strict regulation, indiscriminate groundwater exploitation, its wasteful utilization and land disposal of wastes continued. Research on groundwater use in socio- economic context being relatively small, the highly technical knowledge of the aquifer systems is of relatively little use for practical management purpose. Most of the hydro-geological and groundwater development research has been fragmented, technocratic and relates to groundwater flow and remediation. For practical management practices, it is impertinent to examine people's indigenous adaptive strategies, climate change response etc. However in the present scenario less attention has been paid to these areas. For valuation of groundwater, key elements that may be necessary to consider are:

i) The strategic value of groundwater located near 'high-value' uses such as urban or prime agricultural areas, as opposed to aquifers located in less strategic locations and

ii) Aquifers with high-quality water that is not vulnerable to pollution and the types of uses.

3.6 Management of Water in India

- Water is a State subject under Part VII of the constitution. So, various initiatives on water management including conservation of water in the country are primarily States' responsibility.
- Central Government supports the State Governments in their water management efforts by providing technical and financial support.
- The Union Government has taken many initiatives for the conservation sustainable use of water (especially groundwater) in the country.
- Sustainable groundwater management has become an important issue for the government due to the increasing demand for water resources and the depletion of groundwater levels in many areas.

3.7 Government Initiatives for Groundwater Management

The government has taken several steps to promote sustainable groundwater management. Here are some of them:

a) **Atal Bhujal Yojana (ABY) scheme:** The government has launched the Atal Bhujal Yojana (ABY) scheme to promote sustainable groundwater management. The scheme aims to improve the groundwater management in priority areas of seven states by involving local communities in the process.

b) **National Aquifer Mapping and Management Programme (NAQUIM):** The government has also implemented the National Aquifer Mapping and Management Programme (NAQUIM) to identify and map aquifers across the country. This will help in understanding the groundwater availability and quality in different regions, and facilitate better planning and management of groundwater resources.

c) **Central Ground Water Board (CGWB):** The Central Ground Water Board (CGWB) has been working to monitor and assess the groundwater levels across the country. The CGWB provides technical support and guidance to state governments for the sustainable management of groundwater resources.

d) **Jal Jeevan Mission (JJM):** The government has also initiated the Jal Jeevan Mission (JJM) to provide safe and adequate drinking water to rural households. The JJM focuses on water source sustainability, groundwater recharge, and greywater management.

e) **Har Khet Ko Pani (HKKP):** Har Khet Ko Pani (HKKP) is a part of the Pradhan Mantri Krishi Sinchayee Yojana (PMKSY) with the goal of expanding cultivable land by improving and restoring water bodies. The Surface Minor Irrigation (SMI) and Repair, Renovation & Restoration (RRR) of Water Bodies schemes aim to increase the storage capacity of tanks and revive lost irrigation potential, resulting in improved water use efficiency, groundwater recharge, increased availability of drinking water, and catchment improvement of tank commands.

3.8 Regulation for Sustainable use of Groundwater

The government has developed guidelines for the regulation of groundwater extraction to ensure its sustainable use. The guidelines provide a framework for the allocation of groundwater resources, and promote efficient use of groundwater.

3.9 Use of innovative technologies for groundwater management

The government has encouraged the use of innovative technologies for groundwater management, such as artificial recharge of aquifers, rainwater harvesting, and use of treated wastewater for irrigation.

3.10 Conclusion

Food security and environmental security are the principal global issues of 21 st century. Despite the phenomenal advances made in agricultural technology, there are several regions of the country where food production has either not kept place with the increase in population or has barely kept pace with the increase in population. Although stagnation and decline in agricultural production can be due to political and social reasons, degradation of soil and water resources and lack of appropriate technology to address the basic issue of resource mobilization and management may be the primary factors responsible for low agricultural productivity. Water scarcity and poor water quality are major concern in numerous countries, which mainly depend on agriculture for livelihood of the people. Fresh water availability is already a major factor in sustainable use of resources. The water scarcity is further accentuated by ground and surface water pollution. UNDP warns that world soils and land resources have an important impact on the potential risk of enhanced green house effect. So it is impertinent to note that sustainable water management plays a pivotal role in food security and environmental security in the present era characterized by increasing conflicts over water resources.

References

Chandrakumar and Mukundan. 2006. Water Resource Management, Sarup& Sons.

Datta, P.S. 2005. Groundwater Ethics for its sustainability, Current Science.

Mukherji, A., Villholth, K.G., Sharma, B.R. and Wang, J. 2009. Groundwater governance in the Indo-Gangetic and Yellow River Basins–realities and challenges. IAH Selected Papers in Hydrogeology 15.

Proceedings of the Seminar on Artificial Recharge of Groundwater, December, 1998, Central Ground Water Board, Ministry of Water Resources, New Delhi, 1998.

Romani, S. 2005. Ground water Management: A key for sustainability, CESS papers.

Shah, T., Giordano, M. and Mukherji, A. 2012. Political economy of energy-groundwater nexus in India: exploring issues and assessing policy options. Hydrogeology Journal, 20, 995-1006.

The Citizen's Fifth Report: State of India's Environment, Part-II Statistical Database (eds Agarwal, A., Narain, S. and Sen, S.), Centre for Science and Environment, New Delhi.

Velayutham, M. 1999. In 50 Years of Natural Resource Management Research (eds Singh, G. B. and Sharma, B. R.), Indian Council of Agricultural Research, New Delhi

4

Water Pollution and Waste Water Management

4.1 Introduction

Water pollution is the contamination of water by an excess amount of a substance that can cause harm to human beings and/or the ecosystem. The level of water pollution depends on the abundance of the pollutant, the ecological impact of the pollutant, and the use of the water. Pollutants are derived from biological, chemical, or physical processes. Although natural processes such as volcanic eruptions or evaporation sometimes can cause water pollution, most pollution is derived from human, land-based activities (Figure 4.2). Water pollutants can move through different water reservoirs, as the water carrying them progresses through stages of the water cycle (Figure 4.1). Water residence time (the average time that a water molecule spends in a water reservoir) is very important to pollution problems because it affects pollution potential. Water in rivers has a relatively short residence time, so pollution usually is there only briefly. Of course, pollution in rivers may simply move to another reservoir, such as the ocean, where it can cause further problems. Groundwater is typically characterized by slow flow and longer residence time, which can make groundwater pollution particularly problematic. Finally, pollution residence time can be much greater than the water residence time because a pollutant may be taken up for a long time within the ecosystem or absorbed onto sediment.

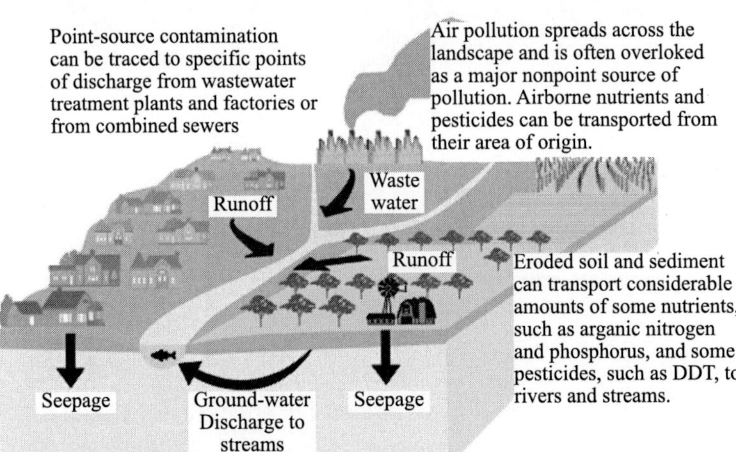

Fig. 4.1: *Sources* of Water Contamination. Sources of some water pollutants and movement of pollutants into different water reservoirs of the water cycle. Source: U.S. Geological Survey

Pollutants enter water supplies from point sources, which are readily identifiable and relatively small locations, or nonpoint sources, which are large and more diffuse areas. Point sources of pollution include animal factory farms (Figure 4.2) that raise a large number and high density of livestock such as cows, pigs, and chickens. Also included are pipes from factories or sewage treatment plants. Combined sewer systems that have a single set of underground pipes to collect both sewage and storm water runoff from streets for wastewater treatment can be major point sources of pollutants. During heavy rain, storm water runoff may exceed sewer capacity, causing it to back up and spilling untreated sewage directly into surface waters (Figure 4.3).

Fig. 4.2: Large animal farms are often referred to as concentrated feeding operations (CFOs). These farms are considered potential point sources of pollution because untreated animal waste may enter nearby waterbodies as untreated sewage.

Nonpoint sources of pollution include agricultural fields, cities, and abandoned mines. Rainfall runs over the land and through the ground, picking up pollutants such as herbicides, pesticides, and fertilizer from agricultural fields and lawns; oil, antifreeze, animal waste, and road salt from urban areas; and acid and toxic elements from abandoned mines. Then, this pollution is carried into surface water bodies and groundwater. Nonpoint source pollution, which is the leading cause of water pollution in the U.S., is usually much more difficult and expensive to control than point source pollution because of its low concentration, multiple sources, and much greater volume of water.

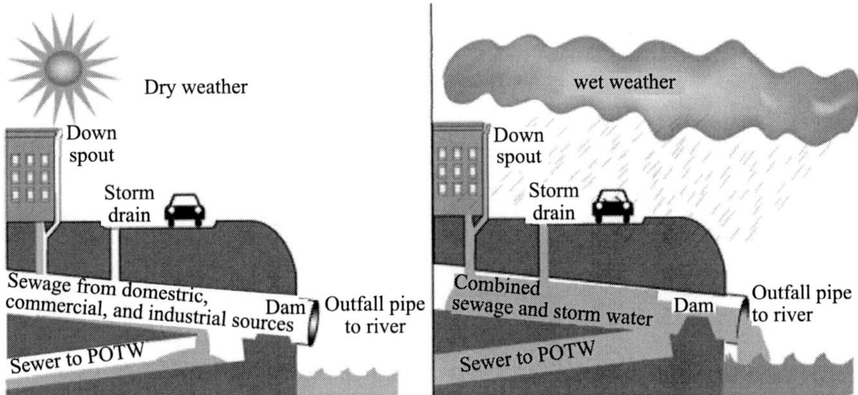

Fig. 4.3: Combined Sewer System: A combined sewer system is a possible major point source of water pollution during heavy rain due to overflow of untreated sewage. During dry weather (and small storms), all flows are handled by the publicly owned treatment works (POTW). During large storms, the relief structure allows some of the combined storm water and sewage to be discharged untreated to an adjacent water body. Source: U.S. Environmental Protection Agency.

4.2 The Causes of Water Pollution

Water is one of the most important elements on Earth when it comes to sustaining life. Unfortunately, it is also extremely susceptible to pollution. This is largely because water is a universal solvent that can dissolve many substances. While this is a wonderful quality that we take advantage of for everyday tasks such as cooking, cleaning and taking medication, it is also the exact quality that causes water to become polluted so easily.

There are many causes of water pollution. Below, we will focus on seven of the major ways that water can become polluted.

4.3 Industrial waste

Industries and industrial sites across the world are a major contributor to water pollution. Many industrial sites produce waste in the form of toxic chemicals and pollutants, and though regulated, some still do not have proper waste management systems in place. In those rare cases, industrial waste is dumped into nearby freshwater systems. The toxic chemicals leached from this waste can make the water unsafe for human consumption, and they can also cause the temperature in freshwater systems to change, making them dangerous for marine life. Finally, industrial waste can cause "dead zones," which are areas of water that contain so little oxygen that marine life cannot survive in them.

Industrial waste from agricultural sites, mines and manufacturing plants can make its way into rivers, streams and other bodies of water that lead directly to the sea. The toxic chemicals in the waste produced by these industries not only have the potential to make water unsafe for human consumption, they can also cause the temperature in freshwater systems to change, making them dangerous for many water dwelling organisms.

4.4 Marine Dumping

The process of marine dumping is exactly what it sounds like, dumping garbage into the waters of the ocean. It might seem crazy, but household garbage is still collected and dumped into oceans by many countries across the world. Most of these items can take anywhere from two to 200 years to decompose completely.

4.5 Sewage and Wastewater

Harmful chemicals, bacteria and pathogens can be found in sewage and wastewater even when it's been treated. Sewage and wastewater from each household is released into the sea with fresh water. The pathogens and bacteria found in that wastewater breed disease, and therefore are a cause of health-related issues in humans and animals alike.

According to the UN, more than 80% of the world's wastewater flows back into the environment without being treated or reused; in some least-developed countries, this figure tops 95%. Harmful chemicals and bacteria can be found in sewage and wastewater even after it's been treated. Households release sewage and wastewater, which makes its way to the ocean, mixing with freshwater and affecting the water quality and marine life. Also, the bacteria and pathogens found in wastewater breed disease, and cause health-related issues in humans and animals.

4.6 Oil Leaks and Spills

The age-old phrase "like water and oil" is used when describing two things that do not mix easily or at all. Just as the saying states, water and oil do not mix, and oil does not dissolve in water. Large oil spills and oil leaks, while often accidental, are a major cause of water pollution. Leaks and spills often are caused by oil drilling operations in the ocean or ships that transport oil. wildlife.

Nearly half of the estimated 1 million tons of oil that makes its way into marine environments each year come not from oil tankers, but from land-based sources like factories, farms and cities. In England and Wales, there are about 3,000 pollution incidents involving oil and fuel each year. Oil makes drinking water unsafe and a substantial amount of oil released into oceans or become river water pollution, will destroy marine life and the ecosystems that support them. What's more, oil reduces the oxygen supply within the water environment. Oil is also naturally released from under the ocean floor through fractures known as seeps.

Fig. 4.4: The Deep-water Horizon oil spill in the Gulf of Mexico in 2010

4.7 Agriculture

In order to protect their crops from bacteria and insects, farmers often use chemicals and pesticides. When these substances seep into the groundwater, they can harm animals, plants and humans. Additionally, when it rains, the chemicals mix with rainwater, which then flows into rivers and streams that filter into the ocean, causing further water pollution.

4.8 Global Warming

Rising temperatures due to global warming are a major concern in terms of water pollution. Global warming causes water temperatures to rise, which can kill water-dwelling animals. When large die-offs occur, it further pollutes the water supply, exacerbating the issue.

There are many everyday ways you can help reduce global warming, which will in turn help lower water pollution. These methods include recycling, carpooling and using CFL bulbs in your home.

4.9 Radioactive Waste

Radioactive waste from facilities that create nuclear energy can be extremely hazardous to the environment and must be disposed of properly. This is because uranium, the element used in the creation of nuclear energy, is a highly toxic chemical.

Unfortunately, accidents still occur at these facilities, and toxic waste is released into the environment. The coal and gas industries are, in many ways, no better. This is one of the major impetuses behind the development of alternative, clean sources of energy, including solar and wind.

In April 2021, Japan discharged contaminated water containing radioactive materials from the damaged Fukushima nuclear plant into the sea. Though the Japanese government claims potential health risks and damage to marine life to be minimal as the waste water have been treated, close monitoring is required to ensure there are no environment effects from the water pollution.

4.10 Marine Dumping and Plastic Pollution in the Sea

Most items collected and dumped into oceans by many countries can take anywhere from two to 200 years to decompose completely. Other sources of waste at sea include plastic and other materials blown or washed from land. Currently, about 11 million metric tons of plastic make their way into the oceans each year. Research has found that should this rate of pollution continues; the amount of ocean plastics will grow to 29 million metric tons per year by 2040. The damage to wildlife habitats and to life on land is incalculable.

4.11 Wastewater

Wastewater is water which physical, chemical or biological properties have been changed as a result of the introduction of certain substances which render it unsafe for some purposes such as drinking. The day-to-day activities of man is mainly water dependent and therefore discharge 'waste' into water. Some of the substances include body wastes (faeces and urine), hair shampoo, hair, food scraps, fat, laundry powder, fabric conditioners, toilet paper, chemicals, detergent, household cleaners, dirt, micro-organisms (germs) which can make people ill and damage the environment. It is known that much of water supplied ends up as wastewater which makes its treatment very important. Wastewater treatment is the process and technology that is used to remove most of the contaminants that are found in wastewater to ensure a sound environment and good public health. Wastewater Management therefore means handling wastewater to protect the environment to ensure public health, economic, social and political soundness (Metcalf and Eddy, 1991).

4.12 Objectives of wastewater treatment

Wastewater treatment is very necessary for the above-mentioned reasons. It is more vital for the:

4.12.1 Reduction of biodegradable organic substances in the environment

Organic substances such as carbon, nitrogen, phosphorus, sulphur in organic matter needs to be broken down by oxidation into gases which is either released or remains in solution.

4.12.2 Reduction of nutrient concentration in the environment

Nutrients such as nitrogen and phosphorous from wastewater in the environment enrich water bodies or render it eutrophic leading to the growth of algae and other aquatic plants. These plants deplete oxygen in water bodies and this hampers aquatic life.

4.12.3 Elimination of pathogens

Organisms that cause disease in plants, animals and humans are called pathogens. They are also known as micro-organisms because they are very small to be seen with the naked eye. Examples of micro-organisms include bacteria (e.g. *Vibro cholerae*), viruses (e.g. Enterovirus, Hepatits A & E virus), fungi (e.g. *Candida albicans*), protozoa (e.g *entamoeba hystolitica*, *giardia lamblia*) and helminthes (e.g. *Vchistosoma mansoni*, *Asaris lumbricoldes*). These micro-organisms are excreted in large quantities in faeces of infected animals and humans (Awuah and Amankwaa-Kuffuor, 2002).

4.12.4 Recycling and Reuse of water

Water is a scarce and finite resource which is often taken for granted. In the last half of the 20th century, population has increased resulting in pressure on the already scarce water resources. Urbanization has also changed the agrarian nature of many areas. Population increase means more food has to be cultivated for the growing population and agriculture as we know is by far the largest user of available water which means that economic growth is placing new demands on available water supplies. The temporal and spatial distribution of water is also a major challenge with groundwater resources being overdrawn (National Academy, 2005). It is for these reasons that recycling and reuse is crucial for sustainability.

4.13 Types of wastewater

Wastewater can be described as.

4.13.1 Definition of concepts and terminology

- **Stormwater Runoff** is water from streets, open yard etc after a rainfall event which run through drains or sewers.
- **Industrial wastewater** is liquid waste from industrial establishments such as factories, production units etc.
- **Domestic wastewater** also known as municipal wastewater is basically wastewater from residences (homes), business buildings (e.g. hotels) and institutions (e.g. university). It can be categorized into greywater and blackwater.
- **Greywater** also known as sullage is liquid waste from washrooms, laundries, kitchens which does not contain human or animal excreta.
- **Blackwater** is wastewater generated in toilets. Blackwater may also contain some flush water besides urine and faeces (excreta). Urine and faeces together is sometimes referred to as night soil. **Sewage** is the term used for blackwater if it ends up in a sewerage system.
- **Septage** is the term used for blackwater if it ends up in a septic tank.
- **Sewerage** system is the arrangement of pipes laid for conveying sewage.
- **Influent** is wastewater which is yet to enter in a wastewater treatment plant or liquid waste that is yet to undergo a unit process or operation.
- **Effluent** is the liquid stream which is discharged from a wastewater treatment plant or discharge from a unit process or operation.
- **Sludge** is the semi-solid slurry from a wastewater treatment plant.
- **On-Site System:** this is wastewater disposal method which takes place at the point of waste production like within individual houses without transportation. On- site methods include dry methods (pit latrines, composting toilets), water saving methods (pourflush latrine and aqua privy with soakage pits and methods with high water rise (flush toilet with septic tanks and soakage pit, which are not emptied).
- **Off-Site System:** in this system, wastewater is transported to a place either than the point of production. Off- site methods are bucket latrines, pour-flush toilets with vault and tanker removal and conventional sewerage system.
- **Conventional sewerage systems** can be combined sewers (where wastewater is carried with storm water) or separated sewers.
- **Septic Tank** is an on-site system designed to hold blackwater for sufficiently long period to allow sedimentation. It is usually a water tight single storey tank.

- **Faecal sludge** refers to all sludge collected and transported from on-site sanitation systems by vacuum trucks for disposal or treatment.
- **Unit Operation:** this involves removal of contaminants by physical forces.
- **Unit Process:** this involves biological and/or chemical removal of contaminants.
- **Wastewater Treatment Plant** is a plant with a series of designed unit operations and processes that aims at reducing certain constituents of wastewater to acceptable levels.

4.14 Characteristics of wastewater

Depending on its source, wastewater has peculiar characteristics. Industrial wastewater with characteristics of municipal or domestic wastewater can be discharged together. Industrial wastewater may require some pretreatment if it has to be discharged with domestic wastewater. The characteristics of wastewater vary from industry to industry and therefore would have different treatment processes-for example a cocoa processing company may have a skimming tank in its preliminary treatment stage to handle for instance spilt cocoa butter while a beverage plant may skip this in the design. In general, the contaminants in wastewater are categorized into physical, chemical and biological. Some indicator measured to ascertain these contaminants include (Peavy, Rowe and Tchobanoglous, 1985 & Obuobie *et al*., 2006):

4.14.1 Physical

- Electrical Conductivity (EC) indicates the salt content
- Total Dissolved Solids (TDS) comprise inorganic salts and small amounts of organic matter dissolved in water
- Suspended solids (SS) comprises solid particles suspended (but not dissolved) in water

4.14.2 Chemical

- Dissolved Oxygen (DO) indicates the amount of oxygen in water
- Biochemical oxygen demand (BOD) indicates the amount of oxygen required by aerobic microorganisms to decompose the organic matter in a sample of water in a defined time period.
- Chemical oxygen demand (COD) indicates the oxygen equivalent of the organic matter content of a sample that is susceptible to oxidation by a strong chemical oxidant
- Total Organic Compound (TOC)

- NH_4-N and NO_3-N show dissolved nitrogen (Ammonium and Nitrate, respectively).
- Total Kjeldhal Nitrogen is a measurement of organically-bound ammonia nitrogen.
- Total-P reflects the amount of all forms of phosphorous in a sample.

4.14.3 Biological

- Total coliforms (TC) is encompassing faecal coliforms as well as common soil microorganisms, and is a broad indicator of possible water contamination.
- Faecal coliforms (FC) is an indicator of water contamination with faecal matter. The common lead indicator is the bacteria Escherichia coli or E. coli.
- Helminth analysis looks for worm eggs in the water

4.15 Levels of wastewater treatment

There are three broad levels of treatment: primary, secondary and tertiary. Sometimes, preliminary treatment precedes primary treatment.

4.15.1 Preliminary treatment

It removes coarse suspended and grits. These can be removed by screening, and grit chambers respectively. This enhances the operation and maintenance of subsequent treatment units. Flow measurement devices, often standing-wave flumes, are necessary at this treatment stage (FAO, 2006).

4.15.2 Primary treatment

It removes settleable organic and inorganic solids by sedimentation and floating materials (scum) by skimming. Up to 50% of BOD5, 70% of suspended solids and 65% of grease and oil can be removed at this stage. Some organic nitrogen, organic phosphorus, and heavy metals are also removed. Colloidal and dissolved constituents are however not removed at this stage. The effluent from primary sedimentation units is referred to as primary effluent (FAO, 2006).

4.15.3 Secondary treatment

It is the further treatment of primary effluent to remove residual organics and suspended solids. Also, biodegradable dissolved and colloidal organic matter is removed using aerobic biological treatment processes. The removal of organic matter is when nitrogen compounds and phosphorus compounds and pathogenic microorganisms are removed. The treatment can be done mechanically like in trickling filters, activated sludge methods rotating biological contactors (RBC) or non-mechanically like in anaerobic treatment, oxidation ditches, stabilization ponds etc.

4.15.4 Tertiary treatment or advance treatment

It is employed when specific wastewater constituents which cannot be removed by secondary treatment must be removed. Advance treatment removes significant amounts of nitrogen, phosphorus, heavy metals, biodegradable organics, bacteria and viruses. Two methods can be used effectively to filter secondary effluent-traditional sand (or similar media) filter and the newer membrane materials. Some filters have been improved, and both filters and membranes also remove helminths. The latest method is disk filtration which utilizes large disks of cloth media attached to rotating drums for filtration (FAO, 2006). At this stage, disinfection by the injection of Chlorine, Ozone and Ultra Violet (UV) irradiation can be done to make water meet current international standards for agricultural and urban re-use.

4.16 Methods of wastewater treatment

There are conventional and non-conventional wastewater treatment methods which have been proven and found to be efficient in the treatment of wastewater. Conventional methods compared to non-conventional wastewater treatment methods has a relatively high level of automation. Usually have pumping and power requirements. They require skilled labour for operation and maintenance of the system.

4.16.1 Conventional methods

Examples of conventional wastewater treatment methods include activated sludge, trickling filter, rotating biological contactor methods. Trickling filters and Rotating Biological Contactors are temperature sensitive, remove less BOD, and trickling filters cost more to build than activated sludge systems. Activated sludge systems are much more expensive to operate because energy is needed to run pumps and blowers (National Programme on Technology Enhanced Learning (NPTEL), 2010).

These methods are discussed in detail in the subsequent sections.

4.16.1.1 Activated sludge

Activated sludge refers to biological treatment processes that use a suspended growth of organisms to remove BOD and suspended solids. It is based on the principle that intense wastewater aeration to forms flocs of bacteria (activated sludge), which degrade organic matter and be separated by sedimentation. The system consists of aeration and settling tanks with other appurtenances such as return and waste pumps, mixers and blowers for aeration and a flow measurement device. To maintain the concentration of active bacteria in the tank, part of the activated sludge is recycled.

Factors such as temperature, return rates, amount of oxygen available, amount of organic matter available, pH, waste rates, aeration time, and wastewater toxicity affect the performance of an activated sludge treatment system. A balance therefore must be maintained between the amount of food (organic matter), organisms (activated sludge) and dissolved oxygen (NPTEL, 2010).

Activated Sludge systems are requires less space compared to trickling filter and has high effluent quality. The disadvantage is that BOD is higher at one end of the tank than the other the microorganisms will be physiologically more active at that end than the other unless a complet mixing activated sludge system process is used. Presently there are 11 activated sludge plants in Ghana, mainly installed by the large hotels (Obuobie, *et al.*, 2006).

4.16.1.2 Trickling filter

It is a growth process in which microorganisms responsible for treatment are attached to an inert packing material. It is made up of a round tank filled with a carrier material (volcanic rock, gravel or synthetic material). Wastewater is supplied from above and trickles through filter media allowing organic material in the wastewater to be adsorbed by a population of microorganisms (aerobic, anaerobic, and facultative bacteria; fungi; algae; and protozoa) attached to the medium as a biological film or slime layer (approximately 0.1 to 0.2 mm thick).

Degradation of organic material by the aerobic microorganisms in the outer part of the slime layer occurs. As the layer thickens through microbial growth, oxygen cannot penetrate the medium face, and anaerobic organisms develop. The biological film continues to grow to such a point that microorganisms near the surface cannot cling to the medium, and a portion of the slime layer falls off the filter. This process is known as sloughing. The sloughed solids are picked up by the underdrain system and transported to a clarifier for removal from the wastewater (US EPA, 2000).

4.16.1.3 Rotating biological contactors

Rotating biological contactors (RBCs) consist of vertically arranged, plastic media on a horizontal, rotating shaft. The plastics range from 2-4 m in diameter and up to 10 mm thick (Peavy, Rowe ad Tchobanoglous, 1985). The biomass-coated media are alternately exposed to wastewater and atmospheric oxygen as the shaft slowly rotates at 1–1.5 rpm (necessary to provide hydraulic shear for sloughing and to maintain turbulence to keep solid in suspension), with about 40% of the media submerged. High surface area allows a large, stable biomass population to develop, with excess growth continuously and automatically shed and removed in a downstream clarifier. Thichness of biofilm may reach 2-4 mm depending on the strength of wastewater and the rotational speed of the disk. RBC systems are relatively new, though it appeared to be best suited to treat municipal wastewater (Peavy, Rowe ad Tchobanoglous, 1985), they have been installed in many petroleum facilities because of their ability to quickly recover from upset conditions (Schultz, 2005). The RBC system is easily expandable should the need arise, and RBCs are also very easy to enclose should volatile organic content containment become necessary. RBCs have relatively low power requirements and can even be powered by compressed air which can also aerate the system. They follow simple operating procedures and thus require a moderately skilled labour. RBCs are however capital intensive to install and sensitive to temperature.

4.16.1.4 Membrane bioreactors

This method performs more than just one treatment step. Membrane bioreactor (MBR) systems are unique processes, which combine anoxic- and aerobic-biological treatment with an integrated membrane system that can be used with most suspended-growth, biological wastewater-treatment systems.

Wastewater is screened before entering the biological treatment tank. Aeration within the aerobic-reactor zone provides oxygen for biological respiration and maintains solids in suspension. MBR relies on submerged membranes to retain active biomass in the process. This allows the biological process to operate at longer than normal sludge ages (typically 20-100 days for a MBR) and to increase mixed-liquor, suspended-solids (MLSS) concentrations (typically 8,000-15,000 mg/l) for more effective removal of pollutants. High MLSS concentrations reduce biological-volume requirements and the associated space needed to only 20-30% of conventional biological processes.

4.16.2 Non-conventional methods

These are low-cost, low-technology, less sophisticated in operation and maintenance biological treatment systems for municipal wastewater. Although these systems are land intensive by comparison with the conventional high-rate biological processes, they are often more effective in removing pathogens and do so reliably and continuously if system is properly designed and not overloaded (FAO, 2006). Some of the non-conventional methods include stabilization ponds, constructed wetlands, oxidation ditch, soil aquifer treatment.

4.16.2.1 Waste stabilization ponds

Waste Stabilization Ponds are man-made, shallow basins which comprise of a single series or several series of anaerobic, facultative or maturation ponds. This is a low-technology treatment process with 4 or 5 ponds of different depths with different biological activities. Treatment of the wastewater occurs as constituents are removed by sedimentation or transformed by biological and chemical processes (National Academy, 2005).The anaerobic ponds are mainly designed for the settling and removal of suspended solids as well as the breakdown of some organic matter (BOD5). In facultative ponds, organic matter is further broken down to carbon dioxide, nitrogen and phosphorous by using oxygen produced by algae in the pond. Maturation ponds usually remove nutrients and pathogenic microorganisms, thus primary treatment occurs in anaerobic ponds while secondary and tertiary treatment occurs in facultative and maturation ponds respectively (Awuah, 2002). Anaerobic ponds are usually between 2-5 m deep and receive high organic loads equivalent to 100g BOD5 and m3/d leading to anaerobic conditions throughout the pond (Mara *et al.*, 1992). If properly designed, anaerobic ponds can remove 60% of BOD5 at 200 C. Facultative ponds are 1-2 m deep and usually receive the effluent from an anaerobic pond. In some designs, they receive raw wastewater acting as primary facultative pond. In facultative ponds organic loads are lower and allows for algal growth which accounts for the dark green colour of wastewater. Algae and aerobic bacteria generate oxygen which breaks down BOD5. Good wind velocity generates mixing of wastewater in ponds thus leading to uniform mixing of BOD5, oxygen, bacteria and algae which better stabilizes waste.

Maturation ponds are usually shallow ponds of about 1.0-1.5 m deep allowing aerobic conditions in for the treatment of facultative pond effluents. Further reduction of organic matter, nutrients and pathogenic microorganisms occurs here. Algal population in maturation ponds is more diverse and removal of nitrogen and ammonia is more prominent.

4.16.2.2 Constructed wetlands

Constructed Wetlands (CW's) are planned systems which are designed and constructed to employ wetland vegetation to assist in treating wastewater in a more controlled environment than occurs in natural wetlands (Kayombo *et al.*, 2000). They are an ecofriendly and a suitable alternative for secondary and tertiary treatment of municipal and industrial wastewater. They are suitable for the removal of organic materials, suspended solids, nutrients, pathogens, heavy metals and toxic pollutants. They are not ideal for the treatment of raw sewage, pre-treatment of industrial wastewater to maintain the biological balance of the wetland ecosystem.

There are two types of CW's namely Free Water Surface (FWS) and Subsurface Flow (SSF) systems. As the name suggests, with FWS, water flows above the ground and plants are rooted in the sediment layer below the water column. With SSF, water flows through a porous media such as gravels in which the plants are rooted. From a public health perspective, SSF should be used in primary treatment of wastewater because there is no direct contact of wastewater with atmosphere.

The SSF is mostly anoxic or anaerobic as oxygen supplied by the roots of plants is used up in biofilm growth and as such does not reach the water column. The flow of water in SSF can be horizontal or vertical (Kayombo *et al.*, 2000). FWS are suitable for treating secondary and tertiary effluents and also providing habitat due to aerobic conditions at and near the surface of the water. The condition at the bottom sediment is however anoxic. Wetlands plants or macrophytes utilized in CW's include Cattails (*Typha latifolia* sp), Scirpus (Bulrus), Lemna (duckweed), *Eichornia crassipes* (water hyacinth), *Pistia stratiotes* (water lettuce) *Hydrocotyle* spp. (pennywort), Phragmites (reed) have been known and used in constructed wetlands.

4.16.2.3 Oxidation ditches

An oxidation ditch is a modified activated sludge biological treatment process that utilizes hydraulic retention time of 24 - 48 hours, and a sludge age of 12 - 20 days. to remove biodegradable organics. Oxidation ditches are typically complete mix systems, but can be modified. Typical oxidation ditch treatment systems consist of a single or multichannel configuration within a ring, or oval. Preliminary treatment, such as bar screens and grit removal, normally precedes the oxidation ditch. Primary settling prior to an oxidation ditch is sometimes practiced and tertiary filters may be required after clarification, depending on the effluent requirements. Disinfection is required and reaeration may be necessary prior to final discharge. Horizontally or vertically mounted aerators provide circulation, oxygen transfer, and aeration in the ditch. Flow to the oxidation ditch is aerated and mixed with return sludge from a secondary clarifier. The mixing process entrains oxygen into the mixed liquor to foster microbial growth and the motive velocity ensures contact of microorganisms with the influent. Aeration increases dissolved oxygen concentration but decreases as biomass takes up oxygen during mixing in the ditch. Solids also remain in suspension during circulation (USEPA, 2000).

4.16.2.4 Soil aquifer treatment

Soil matrix has quite a high capacity for treatment of normal domestic sewage, as long as capacity is not exceeded. Partially-treated sewage effluent is allowed to infiltrate in controlled conditions to the soil. The unsaturated or "vadose" zone then acts as a natural filter and can remove essentially all suspended solids, biodegradable materials, bacteria, viruses, and other microorganisms. Significant reductions in nitrogen, phosphorus, and heavy metals concentrations can also be achieved. After the sewage, treated in passage through the vadose zone, has reached the groundwater it is usually allowed to flow some distance through the aquifer for further purification before it is collected through the aquifer. Soil-aquifer treatment is a low-technology, advanced wastewater treatment system. It also has an aesthetic advantage over conventionally treated sewage since effluent from an SAT system is clear and odour-free and it is viewed as groundwater either than effluent. Discharge effluent should travel sufficient distance through the system and residence times should be long enough, to produce effluent of desired quality (FAO, 2006).

4.16.2.5 Faecal sludge treatment and disposal

Sewage sludge contains organic and inorganic solids that were found in the raw wastewater. Sludge from primary and secondary clarifier as well as from secondary biological treatment need to be treated. The generated sludge is usually in the form of a liquid or semisolid, containing 0.25 to 12 per cent solids by weight, depending on the treatment operations and processes used. Sludge is treated by means of a variety of processes that can be used in various combinations. Thickening, conditioning, dewatering and drying are primarily used to remove moisture from sludge, while digestion, composting, incineration, wet-air oxidation and vertical tube reactors are used to treat or stabilize the organic material in the sludge (ESCWA, 2003).

4.17 Waste Water reuse in agriculture

Irrigation with waste water is both disposal and utilization and indeed is an effective form of waste water disposal (as in slow-rate land treatment). However, some degree of treatment must normally be provided to raw municipal wastewater before it can be used for agricultural or landscape irrigation or for aquaculture. In many industrialized countries, primary treatment is the minimum level of preapplication treatment required for wastewater irrigation. It may be considered sufficient treatment if the wastewater is used to irrigate crops that are not consumed by humans or to irrigate orchards, vineyards, and some processed food crops (FAO, 2006). Nutrients in municipal wastewater and treated effluents are a particular advantage as supplemental fertilizers. Success in using treated wastewater for crop production will largely depend on adopting appropriate strategies aimed at optimizing crop yields and quality, maintaining soil productivity and safeguarding the environment. Several alternatives are available and a combination of these alternatives will offer an optimum solution for a given set of conditions. The user should have prior information on effluent supply and its quality. Wastewater effluent can be blended with conventional water or solely used. Heavy metal concentrations in streams used for irrigation in and around urban centres such as Accra and Kumasi have been sometimes found to be beyond recommended levels for irrigation purposed and should therefore may pose a health concern.

4.18 Challenges of waste water management

Waste water management though not technically difficult can sometimes be faced with socio-economic challenges. A few of the challenges are discussed below.

4.18.1 Infrastructure

Most often than not, wastewater infrastructure are not the priority of most politicians and therefore very little investment are made. It is however important to consider wastewater infrastructure as equally important as water treatment plant because almost all the water produced ends up as wastewater.

4.18.2 Pollution of water sources

Effects of wastewater effluent on receiving water quality is enormous, it changes the aquatic environment thus interrupts with the aquatic ecosystem. The food we eat contains carbonaceous matter, nutrients, trace elements and salts and are contained in urine and faeces (black water). Medications (drugs), chemicals and in recent times hormones (contraceptives) are also discharged into the wastewater treatment plant. Discharge guidelines must be strictly adhered to. This will ensure sustainability of water sources for posterity.

4.18.3 Choice of appropriate technology

Because the economy of most developing countries is donor driven, funds for wastewater plants are mainly from donors. For this reason, they tend to propose the technology which should be adopted. For this reason, when the beneficiaries, take over the facility, its management of the operations and maintenance of parts become quite challenging as the technical expertise, power requirements etc are not sustainable.

4.18.4 Sludge production

Treatment of wastewater results in the production of sewage sludge. There must be a reliable disposal method. If it must be used in agriculture, then the risks involved must be taken into consideration. Due to the presence of heavy metals in wastewater, it is sometimes feared that agricultural use may lead to accumulation of heavy metals in soils thereby contaminating of yields.

4.18.5 Re-Use

Effluents which meet discharge standards could be used for agricultural purposes such as aquaculture or for irrigation of farmlands. The challenge however is that if wastewater treatment plants are not managed and continuously monitored to ensure good effluent quality, reuse becomes risky.

4.19 Conclusion

Wastewater is and will always be with us because we cannot survive without water. When water supplied is used for the numerous human activities, it becomes contaminated or its characteristics is changed and therefore become wastewater. Wastewater can and must be treated to ensure a safe environment and foster public health. There are conventional and non-conventional methods of wastewater treatment and the choice of a particular method should be based on factors such as characteristics of wastewater whether it from a municipality or industry (chemical, textile, pharmaceutical etc.), technical expertise for operation and maintenance, cost implications, power requirements among others. In most developing countries like Ghana, low-cost, low-technology methods such as waste stabilization ponds have been successful whilst conventional methods like trickling filters and activated sludge systems have broken down. Effluent which meets set discharge standards can be appropriately used for aquaculture and also irrigation. Though there are a few challenges in waste water management, they can be surmounted if attention and the necessary financial support are given to it.

References

Adu-Ahyiah, M. and Anku, R. E. 2010. Small Scale Wastewater Treatment in Ghana (a Scenerio). Retrieved, 03-10-2010:1-6.

Awuah, E. and Amankwaa-Kuffuor, R. 2002. Characterisation of Wastewater, its sources and its Environmental Effects" I-Learning Seminar on Urban Wastewater Management.

Central Pollution Control Board. 2009. Status of water supply, wastewater generation and treatment in class-i cities & class-ii towns of India, control of urban pollution series: CUPS/ 70 / 2009 - 10, New Delhi: CPCB.

Comptroller and Auditor General of India. 2011. Water Pollution in India, Report No. 21 of 2011- 12, New Delhi: Government of India.

Economic and Social Commission for Western Asia. 2003. Waste-Water Treatment Technologies: A General Review. United Nation Publication.

Hussain, J., Husain, I., & Arif, M. 2013. Fluoride Contamination in Groundwater of Central Rajasthan, India, and its toxicity in rural habitants. Toxicological & Environmental Chemistry, 95(6), 1048-1055.

Ministry of Environment, Forest and Climate Change, http://envfor.nic.in/division/waterpollution [Accessed May 17, 2017.

Ratnapriya, E. A. S. K., Mowjood, M I M, De Silva, R P, and Dayawansa, N D K. 2009. Evaluation of constructed wetlands for efficiency of municipal solid waste leachate treatment in Sri Lanka" Presentation at DAAD_GAWN Alumni Expert Seminar, March 2010.

5

Drought Forecasting and Management

5.1 Introduction

Out of the many climatic events that influence the earth's environmental fabric, drought is perhaps the one that is most linked with desertification. Drought is a natural hazard originating from a deficiency of precipitation that results in a water shortage for some activities or some groups and is often associated with other climatic factors (such as high temperatures, high winds and low relative humidity) that can aggravate the severity of the event. Drought differs from aridity in that the latter is restricted to low rainfall regions and is a permanent feature of the climate. Drought occurrences are common in virtually all climatic regimes.

Widespread and severe drought conditions in Asia, Latin America and the Caribbean in 2000 have raised serious concerns about the continuing vulnerability of the world community to extended periods of droughts and water shortages. In 2000, major droughts affected much of south-eastern Europe, the Middle East, and the area through central Asia to northern China. Especially hard hit was Afghanistan, Bulgaria, Iraq and the Islamic Republic of Iran and parts of China. In North America, months of above-average temperature coincided with below-normal precipitation through northern Mexico and much of the southern and western regions of the USA, leading to one of the worst wildfires in the past 50 years.

By August 2001, much of Western Asia, Central Asia, and the Middle East was suffering the third year of a continuing drought that severely reduced many countries' crop yields. The countries most affected were Afghanistan, India, Islamic Republic of Iran, Pakistan, and Tajikistan.

Drought disrupts cropping programs, reduces breeding stock, and threatens permanent erosion of the capital and resource base of farming enterprises. Continuous droughts stretching over several years in different parts of the world in the past significantly affected productivity and national economies. In addition, the risk of serious environmental damage, particularly through vegetation loss and soil erosion, as has happened in the Sahel during the 70s, has long term implications for the sustainability of agriculture. Bushfires and dust storms often increase during the dry period.

5.2 Drought - the concept

In any discussion on the preparedness and management strategies for natural hazards, it is necessary to understand first the basic concepts underlying the hazard under discussion. Hence, a brief discussion of the concept of droughts is presented here.

Drought is considered by many to be the most complex but least understood of all natural hazards, affecting more people than any other hazard (Hagman, 1984). However, there remains much confusion within the scientific and policy communities about its characteristics. It is precisely this confusion that explains, to some extent, the lack of progress in drought preparedness in most parts of the world.

Drought is an insidious hazard of nature. Although it has scores of definitions, it originates from a deficiency of precipitation over an extended period of time, usually a season or more. This deficiency results in a water shortage for some activity, group, or environmental sector. Drought should be considered relative to some long-term average condition of balance between precipitation and evapotranspiration in a particular area, a condition often perceived as "normal".

Drought is a slow-onset, creeping natural hazard that is a normal part of climate for virtually all regions of the world; it results in serious economic, social, and environmental impacts (Wilhite, 2000). Drought onset and end are often difficult to determine, as is its severity. Drought severity is dependent not only on the duration, intensity and spatial extent of a specific drought episode, but also on the demands made by human activities and vegetation on a specific region's water supply.

The impacts of drought are largely non-structural and spread over a larger geographical area than are damages from other natural hazards. The non-structural characteristic of drought impacts has certainly hindered the development of accurate, reliable, and timely estimates of severity and, ultimately, the formulation of drought preparedness plans by most governments.

Drought risk is a product of a region's exposure to the natural hazard and its vulnerability to extended periods of water shortage (Wilhite, 2000). If nations and regions are to make progress in reducing the serious consequences of drought, they must improve their understanding of the hazard and the factors that influence vulnerability.

5.3 Early Warning and Forecasting of Drought

Drought in the Indian region can be monitored from the progress of onset and withdrawal of southwest monsoon. Weather forecasts broadly can be classified into three categories viz., (i) short range forecast (validity for less than 3 days), (ii) medium range forecast (validity from 3-10 days period), and (iii) long range forecast (validity for more than 10 days). These forecasts are issued by the India Meteorological Department through All India Radio, Doordarshan, private channels and various Newspapers. The National Centre for Medium Range Weather Forecast in the department of Science and Technology disseminates weather related information through its network of 82 Agromet Advisory Service (AAS) units located mainly in State Agricultural Universities and ICAR institutes. The ICAR funded All India Coordinated Research Project on Agrometeorology is operative at 22 centres in the country. The main objectives of this project are: characterization of climate, crop-weather relations, crop weather modelling, weather related forewarning of incidence of diseases and pests and agro advisory service to the farmers. Some private companies are also collecting and trading weather information to bankers, insurance and forward trading agencies.

5.4 Risk Management versus Crisis Management

The traditional approach to drought management has been reactive, relying largely on crisis management. This approach has been ineffective because response is untimely, poorly coordinated, and poorly targeted to drought-stricken groups or areas. In addition, drought response is post-impact and relief tends to reinforce existing resource management methods. It is precisely these existing resource management practices that have often increased societal vulnerability to drought. The provision of drought relief only serves to reinforce the status quo in terms of resource management. Many governments and others now understand the fallacy of crisis management and are striving to learn how to employ proper risk management techniques to reduce societal vulnerability to drought and, therefore, lessen the impacts associated with future drought events.

As vulnerability to drought has increased globally, greater attention has been directed to reducing risks associated with its occurrence through the introduction of planning to improve operational capabilities (i.e., climate and water supply monitoring, building institutional capacity) and mitigation measures that are aimed at reducing drought impacts. In the past, when a natural hazard event and resultant disaster has occurred, governments have followed with impact assessment, response, recovery, and reconstruction activities to return the region or locality to a pre-disaster state. Little attention has been given to preparedness, mitigation, and prediction/early warning actions (i.e., risk management) that could reduce future impacts and lessen the need for government intervention in the future.

5.5 Drought Preparedness

A key point of dealing with droughts is drought preparedness. However the hydrological cycle leads to shortsighted decision making. People tend to assume that plentiful water supplies are the norm, when occasional droughts are inevitable.

The methodology for drought preparedness planning has been developed in the United States. This methodology, a 10-step drought planning process, has been used by many states in the United States and also by several foreign governments. The purpose of the planning process is to derive a plan that is dynamic, reflecting the changing government policies, technologies, and natural resource management practices. The 10-steps in this process are:

- Appoint a drought task force
- State the purpose and objectives of the preparedness plan
- Seek stakeholder participation and resolve conflicts
- Inventory resources and identify groups at risk
- Develop organizational structure and prepare the drought plan
- Identify research needs and fill institutional gaps
- Integrate science and policy
- Publicize the drought plan, build public awareness
- Teach people about drought
- Evaluate and revise drought preparedness plan

The above process is intended to serve as a checklist to identify issues that should be addressed in plan development, with appropriate modifications.

5.6 Drought Management

Drought plans commonly have three major components:

- Monitoring and early warning
- Risk and impact assessment
- Mitigation and response

5.7 Monitoring and early warning

The overall goal of drought monitoring is to provide information that enables and persuades people and organisations to take action to maximise the probability of successful crop production and/or minimise the potential damage to established crops and other assets. In this regard, a reliable assessment of water availability and its outlook for near and long term is valuable information. In establishing the viability of a drought monitoring system, it is important to consider the following:

- An analysis of the risk of the phenomenon and its likely effect on agricultural production.
- Ensuring that the agricultural community has the ability to make use of the early warning system.
- Scientific assessment of the warning situation are the useful techniques for forecasting the phenomena and adequate real time data to enable these techniques to be used.
- A review of the communication systems to ensure timely dissemination of the message to the users.

Primary objectives of a drought monitoring committee are to:

- Adopt a workable definition of drought that could be used to phase in and phase out levels of govt action in response to drought. In many instances, it may be necessary to apply several definitions that are impact or sector specific.
- Establish drought management areas.
- Develop a drought monitoring system. Coordinate and integrate the analysis so decision makers and public receive early warnings of emerging drought conditions.
- Inventory data quantity and quality from current observation networks.
- Determine data needs of primary users.
- Develop and/or modify current data and information delivery systems.

5.8 Components of drought information

The collection, analysis and dissemination of data and information on droughts will vary according to each country's infrastructure. There are a number of components that can be considered essential in the presentation of a comprehensive picture of droughts in a given region. These include information on:

- Timing of droughts
- Drought intensity
- Drought duration
- Spatial extent of a specific drought episode
- Analysis of the risk of the phenomenon and its likely effect on agricultural production.

A short description of each of these components is presented below.

5.9 Timing of droughts

As mentioned earlier, it is difficult to define the onset of droughts as it is a creeping phenomenon. However, some attempts have been made to define the onset of droughts. According to the British Meteorological Office (Crowe, 1971), an absolute drought begins when at least 15 consecutive days have gone by with less than 0.25 mm of rainfall on all days and a "dry spell" is a period of at least 15 consecutive days none of which has received 1 mm or more. Other definitions of the onset of droughts have been developed using drought indices, which are described in the next section. In addition to precipitation data, it is important to take into account the soil type, soil water holding capacity, and the specific cropping situation to which the information is to be applied.

5.10 Drought intensity

There is a number of ways to provide information on the drought intensity:

a) **Presentation of current rainfall data along with long-term average rainfall:** This is the simplest means of presenting information on drought intensity and is used frequently in many agrometeorological bulletins around the world. Information is presented in either a tabular form or a graphic format. Presentation of monthly totals of rainfall along with long-term average rainfall at representative locations is quite common to describe the drought intensity. While the information presented provides a bird's eye view of drought intensity, it is difficult to understand the spatial nature of droughts from the information provided. Also, when monthly rainfall totals are used, it is difficult to clearly discern the exact nature of the dry spell within the month.

b) **Presentation of current rainfall as a percentage of long-term average rainfall:** The percent of normal precipitation is one of the simplest measurements of rainfall for a location and is calculated by dividing actual precipitation by normal precipitation -- typically considered to be a 30-year mean-and multiplying by 100%. Depending upon the need, it can be computed for either a single month or number of months or a whole year. Ideally, one should be able to compute this for the cropping season (taking into account the dates of sowing and harvesting of crops), but the computation of long-term normal in this case could be a bit cumbersome, especially if there are missing data of daily rainfall.

As Hayes (1999) explained, one of the disadvantages of using the percent of normal precipitation is that the mean, or average, precipitation is often not the same as the median precipitation, which is the value exceeded by 50% of the precipitation occurrences in a long-term climate record. The reason for this is that precipitation on monthly or seasonal scales does not have a normal distribution. Use of the percent of normal comparison implies a normal distribution where the mean and median are considered to be the same.

c) **Using different thresholds of current rainfall as a percentage of long-term average rainfall:** Based on experience with previous droughts and the impacts caused by rainfall deficiency exceeding certain thresholds, some countries such as India use different thresholds of current rainfall as a percentage of long-term average rainfall to delineate the intensity of drought in different parts of the country. If the current rainfall in a given meteorological subdivision exceeds the Long-Period Average (LPA) by 20%, the subdivision is deemed to have received excess rainfall. Threshold values of +19 to -19% of LPA are considered as normal while current rainfall falling within -20 to - 59% of LPA would categorize a subdivision as "deficient". When the threshold value falls below - 60% of LPA, rainfall in a subdivision is considered "scanty".

For example, in 1999, rainfall for India was 95.5% of the Long Period Average (LPA) rainfall, but seven out of the 35 meteorological subdivisions in the country received deficient rainfall i.e., 20% to 59% below the normal rainfall. In other words, some 8.1% of the country was affected by droughts in 1999. Rainfall in 2000 was 92% of the LPA and again seven meteorological subdivisions received deficient rainfall.

d) **Computing drought indices and using the indices in a comparative mode to depict drought intensities:** Drought indices have been developed from known values of selected parameters to present a quantitative description of droughts. Following are some of the most commonly used drought indices around the world.

The decile approach (Coughlan, 1987) used in Australia - Palmer Drought Severity Index (Palmer, 1965) used in the United States - Crop Moisture Index (Palmer, 1968) used in the United States - The Standardized Precipitation Index (McKee *et al.* 1993) which has gained popularity and is being used in many countries.

The decile approach: The decile approach (Gibbs and Maher, 1967) is a non-parametric method to describe the distribution of rainfall totals. Annual rainfall totals for a long series of years are arranged in an ascending order (from lowest to highest) and are then split into 10 equal groups. The first group would be in decile range one, the second group in decile range two etc., In other words, deciles are used to give an element a ranking. It is possible in a decile rainfall map to show whether the rainfall is above average, average or below average for the time period and for the area chosen.

The drought maps highlight areas considered to be suffering from a serious or severe rainfall deficiency. In Australia, these classes are assigned by first examining rainfall periods of three months or more for selected places to see whether they lie below the 10th percentile (lowest 10% of records). The terms serious and severe are defined by:

Serious rainfall deficiency: Rainfall lies above the lowest five per cent of recorded rainfall but below the lowest ten per cent (decile 1 value) for the period in question, - Severe rainfall deficiency: - rainfall is among the lowest five per cent for the period in question.

Once an area has been classified, it remains in the severe/serious deficiency category of the review until the deficiency is removed. Rainfall deficiency is considered removed if it exceeds the third decile and is less than the seventh decile.

Palmer Drought Severity Index: The Palmer Drought Severity Index (PDSI), based on the concept of a hydrological accounting system, relates drought severity to the accumulated weighted differences between actual precipitation and the precipitation requirement of evapotranspiration (Palmer, 1965). The PDSI is calculated based on precipitation and temperature data, as well as the available soil water content. From the inputs, all the basic terms of the water balance equation can be determined, including evapotranspiration, soil recharge, runoff, and moisture loss from the surface layer. The objective of this index was to provide measurements of moisture conditions that were standardized so that comparisons using the index could be made between locations and between months (Palmer, 1965). Drought conditions indicated by different PDSI values are as follows:

The Palmer Index is most effective in determining long term drought-a matter of several months-and is not as good with short-term forecasts (a matter of weeks). The Palmer Index is popular and has been widely used for a variety of applications across the United States. It is most effective measuring impacts sensitive to soil moisture conditions, such as agriculture (Willeke *et al.* 1994). It has also been useful as a drought monitoring tool and has been used to trigger actions associated with drought contingency plans (Willeke *et al.* 1994). Alley (1984) identified three positive characteristics of the Palmer Index that contribute to its popularity:

- It provides decision makers with a measurement of the abnormality of recent weather for a region.
- It provides an opportunity to place current conditions in historical perspective.
- It provides spatial and temporal representations of historical droughts.

There are also several significant limitations of the Palmer Index for monitoring drought. These include no inherent time scale (i.e., shorter length droughts may not be detected or may be underestimated in severity), the tendency to treat all precipitation as rainfall so that snowfall, snow cover, and frozen ground are not accounted for, making real-time winter index values of questionable reliability, and the wide variance in the occurrence of extreme and severe classifications of index values, depending on location. It is important for extreme and severe classifications to occur with the same relative frequency in various parts of a country if these values are going to be used in making policy decisions on eligibility for mitigation and response programs.

Crop Moisture Index: The Crop Moisture Index (CMI), developed by Palmer (1968) subsequent to his development of the PDSI, uses a meteorological approach to monitor week-to-week crop conditions. CMI defined drought in terms of the magnitude of computed abnormal ET deficit which is the difference between actual and expected weekly ET. The expected weekly ET is the normal value, adjusted up or down according to the departure of the week's temperature from normal. The CMI responds more rapidly than the Palmer Index and can change considerably from week to week, so it is more effective in calculating short-term abnormal dryness or wetness affecting agriculture. It differs from the Palmer Index in that the formula places less weight on the data from previous weeks and more weight on the recent week. CMI is weighted by location and time so that maps, which commonly display the weekly CMI across the United States, can be used to compare moisture conditions at different locations.

Because it is designed to monitor short-term moisture conditions affecting a developing crop, the CMI is not a good long-term drought monitoring tool (Hayes, 1999). The CMI's rapid response to changing short-term conditions may provide misleading information about long-term conditions. For example, a beneficial rainfall during a drought may allow the CMI value to indicate adequate moisture conditions, while the long-term drought at that location persists. Another characteristic of the CMI that limits its use as a long-term drought monitoring tool is that the CMI typically begins and ends each growing season near zero. This limitation prevents the CMI from being used to monitor moisture conditions outside the general growing season, especially in droughts that extend over several years. The CMI also may not be applicable during seed germination at the beginning of a specific crop's growing season.

Standardized precipitation index: McKee *et al.* (1993) developed the Standardized Precipitation Index (SPI) to quantify the precipitation deficit for multiple time scales. In SPI calculations, the long-term precipitation record for a desired period is fitted to a probability distribution. If a particular rainfall event gives a low probability on the cumulative probability function, then this is indicative of a likely drought event. The cumulative probability gamma function is transformed into a standard normal random variable Z with mean of zero and standard deviation of one so that the mean SPI for the location and desired period is zero (Edwards and McKee, 1997). Transformation of all probability functions fitted for different rainfall station data results in transformed variate in the same units. Because the SPI is normalized, wetter and drier climates can be represented in the same way, and wet periods can also be monitored using the SPI. Positive SPI values indicate greater than median precipitation, while negative values indicate less than median precipitation.

SPI represents the amount of rainfall over a given time scale, with the advantage that it also gives an indication of what this amount is in relation to the normal, thus leading to the definition of whether a station is experiencing drought or not. Plotting a time series of year against SPI gives a good indication of the drought history of a particular station. Rainfall of two areas with different rainfall characteristics can be compared in terms of how badly they are experiencing drought conditions since the comparison is in terms of their normal rainfall.

McKee *et al.* (1993) used the classification system shown below to define drought intensities resulting from the SPI.

Table 5.1: Drought conditions indicated by different SPI

SPI	Values Drought intensity
2.0 +	extremely wet
1.5 to 1.99	very wet
1.0 to 1.49	moderately wet
.99 to -.99	near normal
-1.0 to -1.49	moderately dry
-1.5 to -1.99	severely dry
-2 and less	extremely dry

McKee *et al.* (1993) also defined the criteria for a "drought event" for any of the time scales. A drought event occurs any time the SPI is continuously negative and reaches an intensity where the SPI is -1.0 or less. The event ends when the SPI becomes positive. Each drought event, therefore, has a duration defined by its beginning and end, and an intensity for each month that the event continues. The accumulated magnitude of drought can also be drought magnitude, and it is the positive sum of the SPI for all the months within a drought event.

One of the advantages of the SPI is that it can be computed for multiple time scales (i.e., 1-, 2- ,3- . . .72 months), thus allowing for comparisons between time periods. This can be an excellent communication tool to the public and to policy makers. In addition, these various time scales can be useful in assessing effects on different components of the hydrologic system (e.g., stream flow, reservoir levels, ground water levels). The SPI is used widely in the United States and in more than 30 countries on a research and operational basis.

5.11 Drought duration

Information on drought duration depends not only on the onset of drought, but equally on when exactly the droughts end. In some years, it might appear that drought had been relieved through a light shower, but in effect the drought could persist because of a subsequently long dry period. Hence it is important to evaluate carefully conditions that could clearly signal the end of droughts e.g., rainfall above a given threshold, soil moisture recharge that would enable crops to recover etc.

It is important to document the exact duration of droughts as part of the drought records along with other details such as timing of droughts, intensity of droughts, drought impacts etc., because the length of the time the drought persisted is a good indicator of the nature of the problem and relates quite well to the damage suffered by crops, livestock etc.

5.12 Risk and Impact Assessment

Drought produces a complex web of impacts that not only ripple through many sectors of the economy but may be experienced well outside the affected region. To more clearly understand the impacts of drought, the phenomenon should not be viewed as merely a natural event. It is the result of an interplay between a natural event and the demand placed on water and other natural resources by human-use systems. For example, societies can exacerbate the impacts of drought by placing demands on water and other natural resources that exceed the supply of those resources.

Risk is a product of a region's exposure to the drought hazard (i.e., probability of occurrence as described by a region's drought climatology) and societal vulnerability, represented by a combination of economic, environmental, and social factors. Therefore, in order to reduce vulnerability to drought, it is essential to identify the most significant impacts and assess their underlying causes. Drought impacts cut across many sectors and across normal divisions of responsibility of government agencies at local, state, and national levels. These impacts have been classified by Wilhite and Vanyarkho (2000).

Information on drought's impacts and their causes is crucial for reducing risk before drought occurs and for appropriate responses during drought. As part of the drought planning process, it is recommended that a Risk Assessment Committee be established that represents those most at risk from drought. The task of this committee is to determine who and what is most at risk and why. This task is best accomplished through a series of working groups under the aegis of the Risk Assessment Committee. The responsibility of the committee and working groups is to assess sectors, population groups, and ecosystems most at risk and identify appropriate and reasonable mitigation measures to address these risks. Working groups would be composed of technical specialists representing those areas referred to above.

5.13 Short Term Strategy of Contingency Planning

The probable date of monsoon withdrawal in north-west India is second week of September and system is quite weak right from the beginning. The weathermen do not predict good rains particularly in north-west India. The fallout of erratic and subdued monsoon rainfall in various parts of the country on kharif and rabi production is imminent. The success of Kharif, pre-rabi and rabi planning will largely depend on how best the following issues are addressed: (i) low water level in 81 major reservoirs of the country which are life line for providing drinking water, irrigation water and generating electricity, (ii) poor economic condition of the rainfed farmers and additional investment in re-sowing or re-planting and they will not be able to invest on costly inputs for pre-rabi and rabi sowing, (iii) low or no stored water in micro-watershed structures for providing lifesaving, pre-sowing and/or supplementary irrigation for rabi sowing and (iv) probability of occurrence of rainfall in end of September or first fortnight of October. Success of good harvest of kharif crop and rabi sowing particularly in rainfed regions will depend largely upon short term measures. Productivity and production are the most crucial issues for which immediate planning is required:

i) Judicious use of surface and groundwater for drinking and irrigation.
ii) Ensuring availability of quality fodder to animals for the period from September, 2009 to June, 2010.
iii) Livestock management including establishment of fodder/feed depots and cattle camps especially for non-miltching and scrub animals.
iv) Selection of crops, cropping sequences and agronomic practices for drought affected areas.
v) Promotion of subsidiary income and employment generating activities.

vi) Gainful implementation of NREGA, RKVY, NFSM, NHM, RGGVY, BRGF and other schemes.

vii) Deployment of Information Technologies for gathering and disseminating information almost on real time basis.

5.14 Rescheduling of the irrigation rosters

Elaborate rosters are generally prepared by assuming normal rainfall and availability of discharge in the canal systems. However, during excessive rainfall deficit, rescheduling is called upon to optimise use of depleted water supplies and high demand. During field visits in the States and direct interaction with the farmers, it was observed that 40-50% of the canal-tails did not receive water even for one irrigation whereas other tails were lucky in having 2-3 irrigations. Assuring at least one irrigation in each tail will make a lot of difference for saving or sowing the crops on a very large area. This would require determined, motivated and skilled management by the managers and operators of the canal system.

Similarly, within a branch, the tail-enders did not receive any irrigation whereas those located at the beginning of the tail enjoyed 3-4 irrigations. This will also require proper enforcement of modified operation system by the Irrigation Department so that all farmers of a tail get their share equitably and this will also result in over-all higher production. Desilting, repairing, renovation and construction of new conveyance system by utilising opportunities under NREGA, BRGF, MPLAD funds, etc. may be undertaken. In the reservoir-based systems like that of Bhakra, Tehri, Nagarjuna Sagar, etc. extended release of water may be re-planned both for the existing kharif and subsequent rabi season.

5.15 Groundwater utilisation

Bore wells/dug wells energised by electricity and diesel have multiplied in recent years and following points are very important for optimising services of these heavily invested utilities.

i) Efficiency of the electric pumps is higher than the diesel pumps. However, because of the subsidised or free supply of electricity, the farmers do not care for the efficiency of the motors or pump-sets and look for cheaper options in the market. Since supply of power is getting limited year by year, farmers should be advised to go in for more efficient but relatively expensive 16 pumping systems. After all they will be able to irrigate more areas for a given supply of electricity.

ii) Uninterrupted supply of electricity: Frequent tripping of the supply was complained to almost all the teams who visited various States and interacted with the farmers. Frequent tripping leads to repeated irrigation of the same spot whereas rest of the field remained uncovered. Farmers were less interested in 8 or 9 hour supply but are very particular about continuous supply without any break so that they are able to complete the entire field with the limited water supply.

iii) Proper maintenance of the motors and pumping sets to reduce friction by way of greasing and other maintenance should be advised for efficient pumping.

iv) Sharp bends and excessive height of the delivery pipes also yield less water.

v) As per the existing electricity tariffs and diesel prices operational expenditure on irrigation by diesel pumps is 4-5 times of the electric pumps. There are several possibilities to derive maximum benefits by proper maintenance and installation of diesel pump-sets. Ultimately, diesel pumps may be phased out by linking with RGGVY (rural electrification) scheme.

vi) In case of rice, continuous standing of water is required only in the initial 15-20 days so as to suppress growth of weeds. However, later on, irrigating one day after disappearance of water is the most economical and efficient way of scheduling irrigation.

vii) Sowing of cotton, soya bean, maize, etc. on the ridges and furrows and letting water in alternate furrows can save 20-30% water.

viii) Sprinklers for cereal crops like wheat and drip system for widely spaced crops sown in lines like sugarcane, cotton, maize etc. can give an efficiency of 80-90%.

ix) Harvested rainwater stored in unlined tanks and ponds should be used for pre-sowing or first irrigation to ensure uniform germination. Storing this water for later period will result into infiltration and evaporation losses.

5.16 Use of poor-quality water

Rainwater is the ultimate source of surface and ground water resources. Because of deficient and scanty monsoon rainfall in most parts of the country, recharging of ground water is not taking place. Water management issues of current concern, therefore are: (i) less exploitation of ground water for irrigation, (ii) increased concentration of salts in the soil profile and groundwater, (iii) increased concentration of specific toxic ions like fluorides and nitrates in water and (iv) non-availability/less availability of drinking water for animals in natural storage structures such as ponds, lakes, tanks etc.

Studies on groundwater resources indicate that 25 to 84% of the poor-quality waters are also being used for cropping in several states of the country such as AP, Gujarat, Haryana, Karnataka, MP, Rajasthan, UP etc. and most of them are currently under the threat of drought. Based upon climate, soil, water and crop factors, the Central Soil Salinity Research Institute, Karnal has standardized water quality guidelines which must be kept in mind while irrigating the crops using poor quality ground water in drought prone areas. In a normal rainfall year salinity developed in soil due to poor quality irrigation water gets leached or washed. However, this does not happen in a drought year and one must deal with relatively higher salinity levels. Some specific strategies for efficient use of poor-quality water are:

i) Mixed and/or alternate use of limited good quality and underground poor-quality waters for irrigation.

ii) Cultivation of salt tolerant varieties like CSR-10, CSR-13, CSR-27 and CSR-30 of rice; KRL 1-4, KRL 1-9 of wheat, CS-52 of mustard, CSG (8962) of gram.

iii) Farmers having residual sodium carbonate (RSC) rich waters should be encouraged to use this for irrigation judiciously after amending with gypsum or as soil amendment. In order to facilitate quick utilization, it is recommended that gypsum should be kept in baskets (made from bamboo/mulberry sticks) and covered with jute sack and placed under the source of irrigation so that improved water is used for irrigation.

iv) The states of Haryana, Punjab, Rajasthan, Madhya Pradesh, Uttar Pradesh and Andhra Pradesh should therefore, need to take special extension programmes and supply gypsum freely and/or on soft loan term basis to promote use of alkali (poor quality) waters.

v) In the saline areas, if there is no rainfall during August, it is proposed that farmers be advised to give pre-sowing irrigation with saline waters and go in for toria cultivation in September or mustard later on.

vi) The farmers having saline waters may go for Isabgol cultivation as this crop can withstand poor quality saline water irrigation up to EC 8dS/m during the rabi season and give profitable yield. Matricaria is another medicinal crop which can be cultivated even up to soil pH 9.5.

vii) Resorting to dry sowing of mustard followed by irrigation with saline water especially in light textured soils.

viii) There should be national level programme for digging farm ponds to store good quality rain water. Such farm ponds should be sealed using plastic linings or other effective method to reduce seepage losses and conservation of water be taken up at state level. This good quality water can be used conjunctively with poor quality groundwater.

ix) In a sizeable area of Rajasthan, groundwater is also loaded with fluorides and nitrates. Retro-fitting of hand pumps have been designed by state agencies for safe use of these waters for drinking. Immediate efforts are required to install these attachments in all drought prone areas having fluoride and nitrate problem for drinking purposes.

5.17 In-situ rain water conservation

Land shaping (if the soil depth permits), contour cultivation, field/contour bunding, tie ridging, digging of trenches, ridges and furrow system of sowing, raised on sunken beds are important practices for conserving and managing rain water for realising higher productivity.

5.18 Tanks and farm ponds

About 11-37 % run-off is generated even by the delayed monsoon and should be stored in the farm ponds or tanks. These will recharge ground water during normal or excessive rainfall year. Rainwater stored in self-sealing or lined ponds can be used for irrigation if there is long break in the rainfall or for pre-sowing of the *rabi* crops to ensure proper germination.

5.19 Contingent cropping

Selection of crops, cropping sequences and agronomic practices are very important. Relatively more drought tolerant, deep rooted and short duration crops, varieties and cultivars are available for different agro-ecological and rainfall situations. If the rain is excessively delayed or main crop has failed cultivation or re-sowing with fodder is the best option. Fodders can be harvested at any stage keeping in view sowing of the next *rabi* season crop.

5.20 Application of fertilizers

Rainfed soils are both hungry and thirsty but due to inherent risk of the un-irrigated rainfed crops, the farmers are always reluctant to invest in basal dose of fertilizers. Top dressing with fertilizer is done generally after establishing good crop stand. Some of the cotton growers are trying application of the fertiliser-solution around germinated seedling with the help of sprayers by removing nozzles. Application of fertilizers and even micro nutrients is very essential to optimise production of rain or irrigation water. Intercropping or mixed cropping with legumes or sowing pulses in cropping sequence also improve soil fertility. Farm yard manure and vermicomposting is specifically important since they enhance water retention of the soil. Phosphorus, sulphur and nutrient solubilising bacteria, fungi, michorhiza and poly-culture are other ways of fertilizing soil. Risk factor can always be taken care of in the insurance of the crops. Soil Health Cards can also be used for optimised application of fertilisers.

5.21 Arrangements of Quality Fodder

Livestock is most resilient livelihood for adapting to drought and other calamities all over the world. Animals can be out migrated, fed on stored fodder or can be liquidated under most adverse conditions. To feed nearly 185 million cattle heads and 97 million buffaloes along with large number of sheep and goats in the prevailing drought condition seems extremely challenging. A large number of unproductive male and female cattle are bound to suffer badly as farmers will prioritize saving their productive animals and all available resources will be deployed for their feeding. During drought, availability of green fodder and natural grasses is drastically reduced leading to infertility of animals which can be restored in 2-3 years only. Even the supply of crop residue, normally used as maintenance ration, is reduced whereas demand is increased due to lesser supply of greens. To mitigate/moderate the situation and to save the animals, following strategy may be adopted in coming months:

i) Reduced sown area under paddy, maize, sorghum (jowar), pearl millet and their curtailed productivity or poor growth of grasses will lead to shortages of fodder and feed.

ii) As the sowing of main rabi fodder crops will start in October-November, catch crop of maize, bajra, sorghum, cowpea, bajra + cowpea, maize + cowpea and toria may be taken up after light showers during August-September.

iii) Rapeseed and mustard, Chinese cabbage and maize may be sown in September for fodder purpose wherever feasible. These crops will be harvested by November to facilitate the sowing of *rabi* cereals.

iv) Under irrigated conditions, sowing of berseem with Chinese cabbage in last week of September may be taken up for early availability of fodder. Senji and lucern may be preferred over berseem cultivation.

v) Dual purpose crops like barley (varieties RD 2715, RD 2035, RD 2522 and BH 75) may be sown in October. One cutting may be taken for fodder at 50-60 days after sowing and subsequent regenerated crop left for grain production.

vi) Oats may be grown in October as multicut fodder to ensure availability of green fodder for longer period.

vii) For quick growth in cereal fodders and higher crude protein contents, application of urea as foliar spray may be taken up.

viii) Looking to scarcity of crop residues, burning of paddy straw and stubbles should not be allowed in Punjab, Haryana and UP. A preliminary estimate indicates that about 20 million tonnes of rice straw is burnt in these three states alone which creates problem of environmental pollution. This can be properly harvested, baled, densified and fortified using 4% urea or molasses and transported to areas of fodder scarcity. Standardised machinery for harvesting, baling, densification and fortification is available with Punjab Agro Federation and in the market. Some budget should be earmarked out of the calamity Relief Fund or National Calamity Contingency Fund for implementation of this plan on priority. Perennial grasses like Bhabhar grass (*Eulaliopsis binata*), guinea grass (*Panicum maximum*), hybrid napier, *Dichianthium annulatum*, *Chloris gayana* etc. which grow naturally during rainy season in different parts of the country can also be properly harvested, baled and fortified for animal feeding either at site or transported to scarcity areas. During this year, wheat straw should also not be burnt in Punjab, Haryana and U.P. It should be properly harvested, baled and densified by machinery used for paddy straw. Stover of 21 maize and mustard wherever available should also be transported to fodder scarcity areas. Soybean chaff can be mixed with other fodders up to the extent of 30 percent.

ix) Sugarcane tops and dry sugarcane leaves from sugarcane growing areas may be transported, enriched for crude protein content and fed in scarcity areas. In areas where sugarcane crop is drying due to moisture stress, whole crop can be harvested and used as fodder.

x) If deficit is very serious, sugarcane bagasse and press mud may be treated and transported to deficit areas for survival feeding.

xi) Partially damaged wheat grain may be diverted for feeding to save the productive animals. However, substandard wheat having very high aflotoxin content should be avoided as the same may result in abortion in pregnant animals.

xii) Efforts should be made to increase the production of supplements like UMMB (Urea Molasses Mineral Block) lick, which can be easily transported (as animal chocolate) to be offered to the animals along with crop residues to increase their palatability and digestibility. For utilizing residues of crops which are normally not fed to livestock, the practice of Total Mixed Ration (TMR) should be propagated. Residues of such crops can be incorporated in TMR at 10-15% level.

xiii) Possibility of feeding of tree leaves after lopping and grazing of grasses in forest areas may be explored in consultation with Forest Department.

Pods of trees like Prosopis juliflora can be collected and supplemented as feed source. These pods contain nearly 13% protein and 25-30% sucrose. In Gujarat, these pods are already used upto 30% of the total ration of the animals. Its' leaves can also be used as fodder upto 10% of the ration. Similarly, leaves and fruits of other trees such as Leucaena leucocephala, Ailanthus excels, Prosopis cineraria, Salvadora persica, Acacia spp., Albizia spp. etc. may be collected to supplement protein content in roughages and moderating fodder scarcity.

xiv) Vegetable/fruit wastes may be collected from the market yards and factories processing such foods (like SAFAL). These are generally high moisture content feeds. In the moist form, these could be distributed to farmers around the factories. After sun-drying these could be transported to deficit areas. The nutritive value of these by-products is reported quite high. Apart from providing additional feed resource, such type of recycling also helps in reducing the environmental pollution.

xv) Export of feed ingredients such as oil meals or de-oiled cakes etc. may be suspended temporarily and diverted for surviving the productive animals in drought affected areas. (xvi) Animal camps may be organized along nearby canals like Indira Gandhi Nahar of Rajasthan having adequate drinking water. Fortunately, there is large number of canals in most of the states afflicted by drought-2009. Farmers along the canals may be persuaded to cultivate fodder crops only and may even be compensated suitably.

5.22 Medium and Long-Term Strategy

Medium and long-term strategies should aim at creating resilience or robustness by various mitigated measures productively.

5.22.1 Securing Good Quality Water in Drought Prone Areas

i) Networking of rivers, reservoirs, lakes and other water bodies existing in high rainfall areas which are prone to periodic flooding. Transferred water could be used for ground water recharging and to fill up dried lakes, water storage structures in dry areas whenever such necessity arises. This seems a viable option because the country receives more than one metre average rainfall in a year with lot of inter-regional variation.

ii) Surface stored water may last only for a few years whereas more than 10,000 year old below ground waters have been analysed in Jaisalmer (Rajasthan) by radio tracer technique. Ground water recharge in dry areas with introduced water, in-situ and ex-situ rainwater harvesting will be sustainable provided its quality is retained. Field, farm or contour bunding, treatment of micro-watersheds, contour cultivation, vegetative barriers, gully plugs etc. can go a long way for conserving rainwater.

iii) Less exploitation of ground water by resorting to low water demanding crops, introduction of precision micro-irrigation techniques such as drip and sprinkler methods in overexploited/critical areas and matching water application schedules with critical growth stage concept may be prioritized.

iv) Collection, conservation and proper storage of rainwater for domestic use and for providing lifesaving irrigation is quite effective. Promotion of roof water harvesting, construction of nadis and khadins may be promoted. Periodic desilting and renovation of village ponds, tanks and other storage structures through NREGA, BRGF, MPLAD, IWMP funding provide ample opportunities. Strict implementation of watershed based agricultural development sequenced from ridge to valley in drought prone areas, holds a great promise.

v) Formulation of strict guidelines for judicious use of water for domestic and industrial purpose in all drought prone areas. These guidelines must be backed by proper legal provisions. There is also an urgent need to declare water as a national asset.

vi) Conjunctive use of ground water by installing bore wells in canal command area will increase overall efficiency and sustainability.

vii) Recycling of used/waste waters after proper treatment and reclamation for agriculture, human and animal consumption. The domestic sewage water which is not mixed with industrial heavy metals can be directly used for raising agro-forestry, industrial bio-mass and parks. Waters having high fluoride and nitrate contents particularly in Rajasthan can be purified by using filter assemblies developed by state government agencies. Highly polluted industrial effluents can be used for irrigating forest plantations after working out their chemical composition and tolerance limits of tree species. This will be a safe disposal option because heavy metals will not enter the animal-human chain.

viii) Joint management of forest and arable land in forest fringe area to harness rainfall and minor forest products requires inter-departmental cooperation and coordination.

ix) Diversification into less water demanding cropping systems. Vast range of options is available to make preferred choices.

5.22.2 Perennial and Non-conventional Fodder

i) Deep rooted bushes, trees, grasses and modified plants of cactus are highly drought tolerant and will be a durable adaptation to climate changes. Perennial component of vegetation may be enhanced in arid and semi-arid regions. Improve natural pasture/grazing lands by in-situ rainwater conservation, reseeding, inclusion of leguminous component such as stylo, sirato etc. and introduction of top feed fodder trees and bushes such as *Prosopis cineraria*, *Hardwickia binata*, *Albizia species*, *Zizyphus numularia*, *Colospermum mopane*, *Azadirachta indica*, *Ailanthus excels*, *Acacia nilotica* etc. Experimental evidences indicate that carrying capacity of arid lands can be raised from 0.5 sheep/ha to 7.3 sheep/ha by proper management of pasture lands. The less productive grasses can be replaced by recently developed more productive and drought tolerant varieties of *Cenchrus ciliaris*, *Cenchrus setigerus* and *Lasirius sindicus*.

ii) Introduction of fodder trees, bushes and grasses as rehabilitation option on all kinds of wasted and abandoned lands. Rehabilitation success stories need to be scaled up on large plots in drought prone areas.

iii) Introduction of fodder spineless cactus as alternate source of green fodder especially in arid regions of Rajasthan and Gujarat requires international partnerships. They can be cultivated in very low rainfall areas and are highly drought resistant evolutions.

iv) Up-gradation of productivity potential and quality of non-conventional perennial vegetation of fodder value existing naturally in drought prone areas through selection, breeding, standard management and agronomic practices. Identification and documentation of anti-quality factors in such plants and developing strategies to detoxify such harmful compounds. Technology needs to be generated to remove/reduce alkaloids from leaves of *Prosopis juliflora* which is available in plenty in drought prone areas.

v) Development of fodder varieties of cultivated crops having tolerance for varying degrees of drought. Emphasis should be on dual purpose varieties of pearl millet, sorghum, barley and oats. Improvement work on drought tolerant grasses, bushes and trees should also be undertaken. There is always a shortage of seeds of grasses and bushes. Rigorous efforts will be required to ensure the availability of quality seed of fodder crops in general and grasses and legumes in particular.

vi) Creation of permanent fodder, feed and seed banks in all drought prone areas (a) using residues of crops like rice, wheat, mustard, maize, groundnut, soybean, chick peas, lentil, etc. grown in irrigated areas of Punjab, Haryana and Western U.P., (b) harvesting and collection of perennial vegetation particularly grasses which grow during monsoon in drought prone areas and other areas of the country, (c) leafy meal of fodder trees and (d) potentials of forest land have not been utilized. Each year these fodder bank resources need to be properly baled, densified and fortified at the sites of their production and then transported to the fodder banks established in drought prone areas. Standard technology of baling, densification and fortification using urea and molasses is already available. This needs to be given a practical shape. In case of non-drought years, 31 this material can be used for making compost, raising of mushrooms and/or rearing of earthworms for producing quality organic manure or composts.

vii) Raising drought tolerant perennial grasses, trees and bushes on field boundaries as permanent source of fodder in all drought prone areas. The selected species should have the ability to withstand severe drought, revive quickly and capacity to yield reasonable biomass of fodder value. The priority should be for exploitation of genus Prosopis and Opunita.

Planting of trees and bushes on the boundaries of agricultural fields in drought prone areas will be highly useful as

i) Bio-fence protection against wild animals,
ii) As an alternate source of food, fodder, fuel and income generating products during severe drought,
iii) As vegetative barriers to conserve soil and water,
iv) Moderating effects of drought through moderating micro climate and
v) In some cases serve as shelter belts/wind breaks.

5.22.3 Upgradation and Fine Tuning of Crops, Cropping and Farming Systems

The strategy should include:

i) relooking and up gradation of our knowledge about mixed cropping, intercropping, catch cropping, mixed farming and multi-strata cropping concepts;
ii) promotion of agro-forestry, silvipasture, horti-pasture and sivi-horti-pasture systems etc. through large pilot scale demonstrations in farmer's participatory mode;
iii) agronomic manipulations such as zero tillage, bed furrow irrigation, fertilization, adjusting spacing, soil and water conservation through mulching, use of anti-transpirants/Jal shakti etc. and

iv) development of extra early maturing short duration area specific crop varieties including fodder crops, perennial grasses; bushes and trees. Synergies 33 of forest and arable land especially in the fringe area in terms of transfer nutrients, water, organic carbon etc.

5.23 Creation of Alternate Income and Employment Generating Opportunities in Drought Prone Areas.

Supplementing by non-farm income and employment reduces vulnerability by reducing poverty and dependence on agricultural resources sensitive to weather abnormalities. Landless, assetless, small and marginal farmers are also job seekers in the NREGA. This can be realized in many ways:

i) Promoting subsidiary occupations such as dairying, mushroom cultivation, sericulture, tasar, bee keeping, and value addition of products obtained from dry land crops such as trees, bushes, grasses etc.

ii) Imparting skills and tools for diversified demands for masonry, carpentry, wiring of motors, repairing of engines, tractor and farm machinery.

iii) Promoting cultivation of drought tolerant medicinal and other high value industrial crops and ensuring attractive prices by linking with markets.

iv) Promoting the use of unexploited/under exploited food and feed resources such as edible and forage cactus and genus Prosopis. Some of these crops are already exploited for multiple use in different parts of the world.

v) Small and marginal farmers may be employed under NREGA for creating rain water conservation and storage structures to enhance productivity of their limited land.

5.24 Convergence of Resources and Harnessing Synergies

Requirement of resources during natural calamities is tremendous. There are several innovative, pro-active, flexible, institutionally enabled and decentralized schemes to respond quickly for managing drought. Already sanctioned and released funds of such schemes are very attractive preposition for responding to drought quickly. Some of them are mentioned below for ensuring quick results.

i) RKVY: It is a Rs.25,000 crore scheme with approval of projects decentralized to the states. Subsidy for the purchase of seeds of crops, varieties, inputs, pumping sets etc. can be planned. Various relaxations have already been notified by the Ministry of Agriculture.

ii) NREGA: The current year budget of Rs.39,000 crore provides vast opportunities for relatively likely high demand of employment due to drought. These resources can be used for de-silting of tanks, ponds, other water bodies, canals, repairing or construction of water conveyance systems, field bunding, contour bunding, digging of trenches even on the fields of small and marginal farmers. Digging of farm ponds even for small and marginal farmers should be the high priority of drought adaptations and proofing. Land shaping, levelling of fields, making ridges and furrows or beds and furrows to enhance irrigation and water use efficiency are also permitted in the scheme. Labour for spreading organic manure, mulching to prevent loss of stored moisture could be booked to this scheme.

iii) **Micro irrigation scheme:** Drought managers may focus on popularizing sprinklers, dripper, fertigation etc.

iv) **BRGF:** It is an untied fund and has been used generally for civil works of roads etc. However, it could also be considered for implementing drought contingency activities.

v) **IWMP:** This is about Rs.16,000 crores scheme, common guidelines are available, almost all states have been sensitized in workshops organized by NRAA and its resources can be deployed for managing drought. Livestock based interventions, activities for landless, in situ conservation and harvesting of rain for supplemental irrigation to save crops, farming systems etc. are tremendous opportunities.

vi) **NFSM:** Alternative contingency cropping of boro rice, wheat, etc. can be considered under these resources.

vii) **Artificial groundwater recharging:** It is a Rs.1600 crore scheme of the Ministry of Water Resources. There are about 10 million dug wells in the country, about 40% have dried up and can be recharged with these resources. There are also several other ways of recharging ground water which is an important strategy of drought proofing.

viii) **AIBP:** Lift irrigation schemes, water harvesting by constructing weirs, check dams and conveyance system may be prioritized in the implementation process to alleviate drought stress.

5.25 Conclusion

Drought preparedness and management are effective strategies to reduce risks and therefore the impacts associated with droughts. Preparedness for drought necessitates greater institutional capacity at all levels of government and more efficient coordination between different levels of government. Preparedness also implies increasing the coping capacity of individuals and communities to deal with drought events. Most commonly, there are three components in a drought plan: monitoring and early warning; risk assessment; and mitigation and response. Given the improved tools and technologies available today, it is possible to provide drought information that enables action to maximise the probability of successful crop production and/or minimise the potential damage to established crops and other assets. To this end, information should be provided on the timing, intensity and duration and the spatial extent of droughts. An equally important element of drought early warning systems is the timely and effective delivery of this information to decision makers. To provide effective drought information, there should be improved collaboration among scientists and managers to enhance the effectiveness of observation networks, drought monitoring, prediction, information delivery, and applied research. Such a collaboration could help foster public understanding of and preparedness for drought.

References

Alley, W. M., 1984. The Palmer Drought Severity Index: limitations and assumptions. Journal of Climate and Applied Meteorology, 23:1100-1109.

Coughlan, M.J. 1987. Monitoring drought in Australia. Pages 131-144 In: (D.A. Wilhite and W.E. Easterling with D.A. Wood. Eds.) Planning for Drought: Toward a Reduction of Societal Vulnerability. Boulder and London: West View Press.

IPCC, 2013: Summary for Policymakers, in: Climate Change 2013: The Physical Science Basis. Contribution of Working Group I to the Fifth Assessment Report of the Intergovernmental Panel on Climate Change, edited by: Stocker, T. F., Qin, D., Plattner, G.- K., Tignor, M., Allen, S. K., Boschung, J., Nauels, A., Xia, Y., Bex, V. and Midgley, P. M., Cambridge University Press, Cambridge, United Kingdom and New York, NY, USA.

McKee, T. B., N. J. Doesken, and J. Kleist, 1993. The relationship of drought frequency and duration to time scales. Preprints, 8th Conference on Applied Climatology, 17-22 January, Anaheim, CA, pp. 179-184.

Monteith, J. L.: Evaporation and environment. Proc., Symposium of the Society for Experimental Biology: The State and Movement of Water in Living Organisms, Academic Press, Inc., NY., 19, 205–234, 1965.

Nagesh Kumar, D., Srinivasa Raju, K., and Ashok, B.: Optimal reservoir operation for irrigation of multiple crops using genetic algorithms, J. Irrig. Drain. Eng., ASCE 132, 123–129, 2006.

Palmer, W. C., 1968. Keeping track of crop moisture conditions, nationwide: the new Crop Moisture Index, Weatherwise, 21:156-161.

Wilhite, D.A. 2000. Drought as a Natural Hazard: Concepts and Definitions (Chapter 1, pp. 3-18). In: Wilhite, D.A. (ed.) Drought: A Global Assessment (Volume 1), Routledge Publishers, London, U.K.

6

Plant Bio-regulators: Water Stress Mitigation Strategy in Field Crops

6.1 Introduction

Water deficit stress is a serious and frequently encountered abiotic stress in the terrestrial surface. Its deleterious effects on plant growth and productivity are well documented. Plant responses to water stress are believed to be complex as these operate at various levels of plant organization. Several in-built physiological and biochemical mechanisms provide resistance to plants against stress. An understanding of the processes linked to these mechanisms is vital for optimizing crop growth and productivity under stress. Plants respond and adapt to water stress by altering cellular metabolism, thus invoking stress tolerance. Alteration in endogenous concentrations of growth regulators along with accumulation of osmolytes, modifications in antioxidant cascade, changes in protein profiles and induction of gene expression in plants under stress are important characteristic metabolic changes that invoke stress tolerance at the cellular level. Alteration in endogenous concentrations of plant bio-regulators under stress helps plants through better turgor maintenance and efficient water usage by influencing stomatal functioning, hydraulic conductivity and morphological adaptation. Progress made in plant adaptation to water stress is an outcome of advances made in analytical techniques on endogenous growth regulator analysis and powerful and reliable molecular and genetic techniques.

6.2 Plant bioregulators (PBRs)

The most commonly used plant bio regulators include various plant hormones which affect plant's ability to respond to its environment. Each hormone interacts with specific target tissues to cause physiological responses, such as growth and development. Often each response is the result of two or more hormones acting together. Among them, many hormones can be synthesized in the laboratory for commercial applications. GA and SA are widely used plant hormones that regulate a wide range of metabolic and physiological responses in plants such as seed germination, seedling establishment, stomatal closure, respiration, cell growth, senescence-associated gene expression, responses to abiotic stresses, thermo tolerance, nodule formation in legumes and crop yield. Hence, they are used as PBRs for enhancing plant growth and yield and for particular stress alleviation. However, excess use of SA proves toxic for the plant growth.

6.3 Different classes of plant bioregulators

- Chemical based PBR having redox modulating action.
- Chemical based PBR constituting structural component.
- Hormone based PBR having redox modulating action.

6.4 Effects of plant bioregulators

Any type of chemical, natural or chemosynthetically derived, may have plant bioregulatory action. Plant bio-regulators are readily absorbed by plants. They readily penetrate the living surface cells of most plant parts and seem to move as readily through intact epidermal cells as through injured ones. Synthetic biochemical regulators readily gain entrance to the plant when applied to roots, stem leaves, flowers or fruits. These organs absorb them even though the surface cells of some may be protected by thick walls. After biochemical regulators have been absorbed and have moved to the different parts of the plant, they incite specific physiological responses, which are sharply reflected in or evidenced by the amount and kind of chemical constituents in the plants. Worthy of note is the fact that different types and concentrations of biochemical regulators have been screened for their effects on terpenoid, alkaloid and sterol biosynthesis in tissue cultures. In the cell cultures of Valeriana wallichii and Felia cornucopiae, dimethylmorpholinium bromide 1,1-dimethylpiperidinium chloride (mepiquat chloride) at concentrations greater than 10 ppm reduced valepotriate production but did not affect cell growth. The production of berberine, an isoquinoline alkaloid was stimulated by naphthalene acetic acid (NAA) in Thalictrum dipterocarpum but suppressed in Thalictrum flavum. IAA markedly stimulated the synthesis of solasodine in tissue cultures of Solanum nigrum; however, auxins, especially indole butyric acid (IBA) inhibited alkaloid biosynthesis in Hyoscyamus spp., Datura, Atropo and Duboisia root cultures. Investigators have also evaluated the effects of growth regulators on pollen tube growth, studied the role of various bioregulators on tomato puffiness and stomatal response to bioregulators in vitro in Chrysanthemum. The biosynthesis of anthraquinones has equally been shown to be highly influenced by various bioregulators, whether natural, synthetic or chemical, as indicated by the effects of methyl 2-4-chlorophenoxy acetic acid (MCPA), 2,4-D, 4-chlorophenoxyacetic acid (4CPA), NAA and IAA on anthraquinone production. Generally, bioregulators have been instrumental in understanding morphological and growth phenomena in-vitro. They are potential tools for elucidating biochemical pathways in plants.

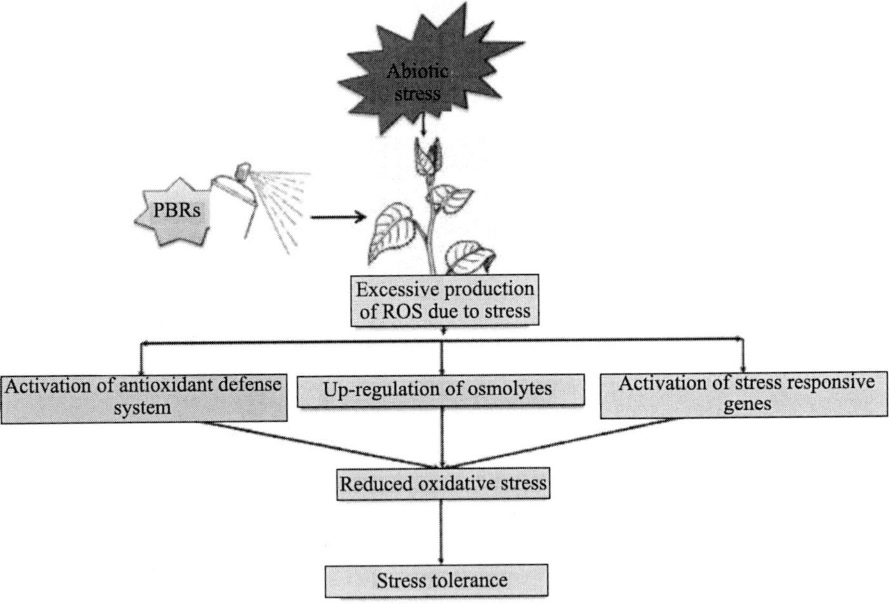

Fig. 6.1: Mode of actions of PBRs

6.5 Benefits of bioregulators

Application at very low concentrations (1 or 2 parts per billion) has the potential to increase food production much more quickly than plant breeding techniques. Also, the beneficial effects of a commercially viable chemical are usually not restricted to a single species and the time-scale involved to achieve a commercially desirable result is often shorter. Some benefits of the use of bioregulators for food production include better weather resistance, lodging control in wheat, cotton, pea, rice, tomatoes and barley; fruit tree shaping; sugarcane maturation and inhibition of natural breakdown in sugar contents of sugarcane and sugarbeet after ripening; strawberry runner control, promotion of formation of biomass, inhibition of transpiration and increased efficiency of water utilisation; enhanced yield and quality and easier harvest of many food crops.

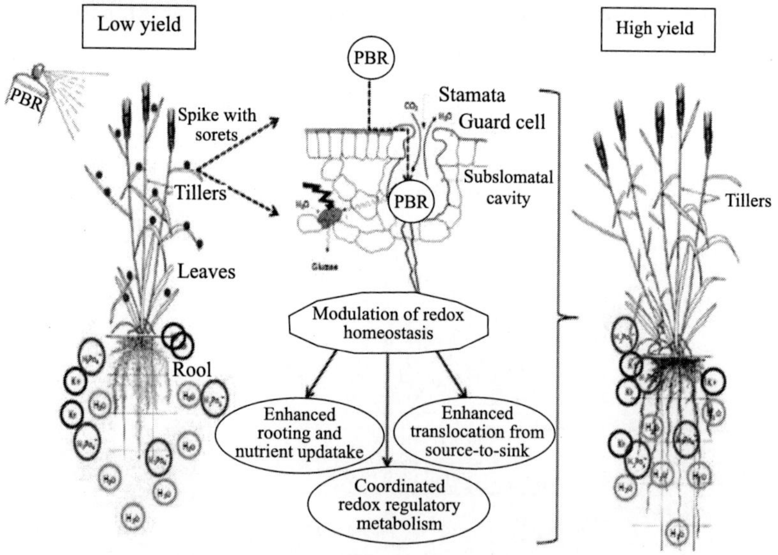

Fig. 6.2: Plant Bio-regulator application and their unified mechanism of action

6.6 Roles of plant bio-regulators in drought resistance

In recent years, a large number of studies have demonstrated that application of exogenous PBRs by seed priming, root irrigation, or foliar spraying is an effective strategy to improve drought resistance by: (1) improving plant antioxidant capacity, (2) promoting plant osmotic adjustment capacity, (3) protecting the photosynthetic system and maintaining plant photosynthetic efficiency, (4) changing the external and internal structure of roots and leaves to improve water absorption and transport, (5) regulating the processes of nutrient and energy metabolism, and (6) regulating the expression of functional genes and the activities of functional proteins.

A. Salicylic acid (SA)

Salicylic acid (SA) is another plant hormone that regulates plant growth and abiotic stress responses. Exposure of plants to water stress leads to serious physiological and biochemical dysfunctions including reduction in turgor, growth, photosynthetic rate, stomatal conductance and damages of cellular components. SA has significant role in controlling abiotic stresses including drought and salinity stress. SA has high potential for improving stress tolerance in agriculturally important crops. However, its utility depends on various factors like concentration of SA applied, mode of application and the stage of plant growth. At low concentrations SA has been found to alleviate abiotic stress and at higher concentrations it induces oxidative stress. Higher tolerance to drought stress was also observed in the plants raised from the grains soaked in aqueous solution of acetyl salicylic acid (Hamada, 1998; Hamada and Al-Hakimi, 2001). It has been suggested that SA-induced drought tolerance is associated with an enhanced antioxidant system. However, very little is known about the molecular mechanisms of SA-induced drought or other abiotic tolerances in higher plants. A few studies have shown that abiotic tolerance induced by SA could be related to the altered expression of the genes encoding osmotin, pathogenesis-related proteins, and heat shock proteins. To explore the molecular mechanisms involved an effort was made by Kang *et al.* (2013). They found that treatment with 0.5 mM salicylic acid (SA) significantly alleviated growth inhibition induced by drought in wheat seedlings by significantly increasing the content of ascorbate (ASA) and glutathione (GSH) due to enhanced transcription of GST1, GST2, glutathione reductase (GR), and mono-dehydro ascorbate reductase (MDHAR) genes. Treatment with SA increased drought tolerance of common bean (Phaseolus vulgaris) and tomato (Solanum lycopersicum) plants. Exogenously applied SA has also been reported to modulate activities of intracellular antioxidant enzymes SOD and POD and increase plant tolerance to environmental stresses. Application of SA alleviated adverse effects of drought stress in wheat plants by increasing improving stomatal regulation, maintaining leaf chlorophyll content, increasing water use efficiency, and stimulating root growth. Leaf senescence is a highly regulated physiological process, allowing the remobilization of stored food from the older leaves to the rest of the plant, during stressful conditions and SA involved in the promotion of drought-induced leaf senescence in Salvia officinalis plants (Abreu and Munne-Bosch, 2008). The results reported by Singh and Usha (2003) revealed that the wheat seedlings subjected to drought stress when treated with SA generally exhibited higher moisture content and also higher dry matter accumulation, carboxylase activity of Rubisco, SOD and total chlorophyll content compared to the untreated plants. Exogenous application of SA also alleviated the damaging effects of water deficit on cell membranes of barley plants and concomitantly increased ABA content in leaves, which might have contributed to the enhanced tolerance of plants to water scarcity. Besides providing tolerance to plants against drought stress, the exogenous application of SA was also found to be effective in providing resistance to the plants against the excessive water stress as was observed in cell suspensions prepared from the fully turgid leaves of Sporobcdus stapfianus. The impact of thiourea in improving productivity of wheat (Sahu and Singh, 1995), showed individual grain weight significantly improved under soil and foliar treatments of TU.

Proteomic data from wheat plants treated with exogenous SA and drought showed that the differentially expressed proteins induced by exogenous SA under drought stress were involved in the regulation of photosynthesis, carbon assimilation, protein metabolism, amino acid metabolism, energy metabolism, redox balance, signal transduction, and other biological processes, suggesting that SA may regulate these physiological processes to enhance wheat drought resistance. In addition, Hussain *et al.* (2020) suggested that the application of acetylsalicylic acid (a derivative of SA) also improved the drought resistance of chickpea by activating the antioxidant defense system. As the main representative jasmonate substances, jasmonic acid (JA) and methyl jasmonate (MeJA) are also endogenous PGRs in higher plants. The combined application of SA and MeJA has been shown to promote the accumulation of endogenous ABA and osmotic adjustment substances and to improve the activities of antioxidant enzymes, thereby improving maize drought resistance.

It is a well-established fact that SA potentially generates a wide array of metabolic responses in plants and also affects the photosynthetic parameters and plant water relations. However, contrary to these observations, a reduction in chlorophyll content was observed in plants pre-treated with SA. Moharekar *et al.* (2003) reported that SA activated the synthesis of carotenoids and xanthophylls and also enhanced the rate of deep oxidation with a concomitant decrease in chlorophyll pigments and chlorophyll a/b ratio in wheat. However in contrast, the transpiration rate decreased significantly in Phaseolus vulgaris and Commelina communis after the foliar application of SA. That decrease in transpiration rate was attributed to the fact that SA induced the closure of stomata. SA was also shown enhance photosynthesis and growth of soybean (C3 plant) and corn (C4 plant) under greenhouse conditions. SA also has capacity of osmotic adjustment by maintaining low MDA contents and decreased Na+/ K+ ratio in leaves. Brassinosteroids enhance tolerance to drought and cold stress by modulations of the expression of drought- and cold-stress marker genes. However, the exact biochemical link between the Brassinosteroids -signal cascade and stress tolerance remain a mystery.

Table 6.1: Application of Salicylic acid on different crops

PBR	**Crop**	**Concentration**	**Type of stress**	**Mode of application**	**Effect observed**	
Salicylic acid	Wheat	0.05 M	Drought stress	Grain presoaking	Enhanced grain yield	Aldesuquy *et al.*, (2012); Kovacik *et al.*, (2009); Noreen and Ashraf, (2010)
	Soybean	10mM	Drought	Foliar Application	Enhanced water Production function, yield	Minhas *et al.*, 2015
	Maize	1μM	Drought	Foliar spray	Enhanced antioxidant capacitance	Saruhan *et al*,(2012); Palma *et al.*, 2013
	Barley	50μM	Drought and salt stress	Soil application	Reduced oxidative damage and Na^{+}/K^{+} ratio in leaves; increased chlorophyll content	Fayez *et al.*, (2014)
	Wheat	0.5mM	Drought	Soil application	Reduced oxidative damage and improved plant growth	Kang *et al.*, (2013)
	Wheat	0.7mM	Drought	Spray (400 l/ha)	Decreased canopy temperature, increased leaf area index and plant growth	Anosheh *et al.*, (2012)

B. Thiourea

Both soil and foliar treatments of thiourea (TU) increased the number of ears and grains/ear, indicating an improved storage capacity. In this context, it is noteworthy that di-thiothreitol, a thiol containing two -SH groups, stimulated carbon dioxide assimilation in the dark up to five-folds. Because of its cytokine-like activity, TU might have also delayed leaf senescence. In maize, foliar spray of TU increased both canopy photosynthesis and photosynthetically active leaf surface during grain filling. Chloroplasts isolated from mature leaves of 30 μM DCPTA-treated plants, as compared with that of controls, showed a 23% increase in the total soluble protein to chlorophyll ratio. This parallels to an observed increase in activated ribulose 1, 5-bisphosphate carboxylase/oxygenase (Rubisco) activity in vitro per unit chlorophyll. The Rubisco activity increased 87% per dm2 leaf area of 30 μM DCPTA-treated plants. Increased Rubisco activity largely accounted for increase in net photosynthesis in DCPTA treated plants. However, intense sink demand for photosynthate and the delayed leaf senescence of older leaves may increase net-carbon assimilation in mature (source) leaves of DCPTA-treated plants. Tolerance to drought stress is enhanced in PGPR inoculated plants. Plants achieve this tolerance either due to the production of IAA, cytokinins, antioxidants and ACC deaminase. Reports are also available regarding role of PGPR in conferring resistance to water stress in plants such as tomatoes and peppers under water deficient conditions. More efforts are needed to investigate the mechanistic approach of PGPR in eliciting tolerance to different stresses. This would improve our understanding of induced systemic tolerance to water stress in modern agriculture.

Table 6.2: Application of Thiourea on different crops

PBR	Crop	Concentration	Type of stress	Mode of application	Effect observed	Reference
Thiourea	Wheat	10 mM	Drought	Soil application	Enhanced phloem loading of sucrose	Sahu and Singh, 1995; Ratnakumar *et al.* (2016)
		10 mM	Drought	Foliar spray	Enhanced growth & seed yield	NIASM (2013)
	Maize	500 and 1000 mg L^{-1}	Sandy soil	Foliar spray	Yield enhancement	Amin *et al.* (2013)
	Brassica	6.5 mM	Salt	Soil application	Maintain plant water homeostasis	Srivastava *et al.* (2013, 2016);
	Potato	250, 500, 750 and 1000 mM	Normal condition	Foliar spray	Enhanced yield & quality of tubers	Mani *et al.* (2013)
	Mung bean	500 and 1000 ppm	Arid region	Foliar spray	Enhanced plant growth and seed yield	Mathur *et al.* (2006)

Table 6.3: Biochemical and molecular mechanisms of thiourea action in different plant species under stress conditions

Mode of Thiourea application	Level of thiourea/stress applied	Plant species	Physiological/Biochemical/molecular mechanism induced	Reference
Seed treatment	10mM + heat stress (10°C higher than control)	Sunflower	Improvement of heat tolerance with the induction of enzymatic and non-enzymatic antioxidants.	Akladious *et al., 2014*
Seed soaking	7mM	Wheat	Further enhancement in the activities of invertases enzymes due to seed soaking in thiourea	Asthir *et al., 2015*
Foliar spray	250 g/ha	B. juncea	Enhanced source strength, sucrose translocation to the developing seed, increased pod photosynthesis and oil biosynthesis	panday *et al.,* 2013
Medium supplementation	6.5mM + 700mM NaCl	B. juncea	Improved water homeostasis of root under salinity stress with the expression of isoforms of aquaporins (PIPs-plant incorporated protectants)	Srivastava *et al.,* 2010

C. Polyamine

Maintenance of the crops in adverse stress conditions without losing the yield is need of the hour, where polyamines can serve an important role. Polyamines are low-molecular-weight polycationic amines occurring ubiquitously in almost all living beings. Apart from being essential for plant development and other physiological processes, they are also involved in modulation of the plant defence to various abiotic stresses. The antistress property of polyamines is attributed to their acid-neutralizing, antioxidant, and cell-wall-stabilizing abilities. There are ample evidences demonstrating that cellular levels of polyamines including putrescine, spermidine, and spermine are elevated at some stage in the stress conditions. Not only the endogenous synthesis but also the exogenous supply of polyamines and genetic transformation with polyamine biosynthetic genes has been found to be involved in stress response in plants.

Table 6.4: Application of Polyamines on different crops

PBR	Crop	Concentration	Type of stress	Mode of application	Effect observed	Reference
Poly-amines	Rice	1mM Spermidine/ 1mM Spermine	Salt stress	In growth medium	Reduced Na^+/K^+ ratio and oxidative damage	Roychoudhury *et al.* (2011)
	Ginseng	0.1-1 mM Spermidine	Salt stress	In growth medium	Prevention of chlorophyll degradation and enhanced enzymatic capacitance	Parvin *et al.* (2014)
	Welsh onion	2 mM Putrescine	Flooding	Soil application	Reduced oxidative stress and improved plant growth	Yiu *et al.* (2009)
	Cucumber	0.3mM Spermine	Salt stress	Foliar spray	Increased activity of SOD, APX, POD; Reduced level of MDA	Shu *et al.* (2013)
	Tomato	1mM Putrescine	Salt stress	Foliar spray	Enhanced antioxidant activity	Slathia *et al.* (2012)
	Soybean	0.4 μM Spermine	Osmotic stress	Soil application	Increased water content and enzymatic antioxidant activities	Radhakrishnan and lee (2013)

D. Gibberellic acid (GA_3)

A hormone imbalance in plant tissues exposed to osmotic stress has drastic effects on plant growth and metabolism. Therefore, exogenous application of growth hormones may be useful to return metabolic activities to their normal levels. Gibberellic acid (GA_3), at certain concentrations, has been shown to be beneficial for the physiology and metabolism of many plants, since it may provide a mechanism to regulate physiology, biochemistry, growth and development as a function of water availability. Gibberellic acid application to the seeds before sowing caused slight changes in growth parameters as well as some physiological and biochemical aspects under water deficit conditions.

Table 6.5: Application of Gibberellic acid on different crops

PBR	Crop	Concentration	Type of stress	Mode of application	Effect observed	Reference
Giberellic acid	Wheat	150 ppm	Salt stress	Seed priming	Decreased Na accumulation	Iqbal and Ashraf (2013)
	Maize	50&100 ppm	Salt stress	Foliar spray	Enhanced nutritional status and improved plant growth	Tuna *et al.*, (2008)
	Tomato	100 ppm	Salt stress	Soil application	Increased water use efficiency and yield	Maggio *et al.*, (2010)
	Wheat	10^{-6} & 10^{-8} M	Nickel tolerance	Presoaking	Decreased electrolyte leakage and MDA content; Increased chlorophyll. proline, CAT, GR, APX, SOD content	Siddiqui *et al.*, (2011)
	Common bean	0.05mM	Salt stress	In nutrient solution	Reduced oxidative damage and enhanced antioxidant enzyme capacitance	Saeidi-Sar *et al.*, (2013)

E. Hydrogen peroxide (H_2O_2)

Hydrogen peroxide (H_2O_2), a major kind of PBR plays an important role in signal transduction for abiotic stress tolerance, although H_2O_2 is toxic at high concentrations. Some authors suggested that the application of H_2O_2 at low concentrations could improve plant tolerance to abiotic stresses such as drought, and heavy metal stresses. Hydrogen peroxide induced increases in antioxidant enzyme activities of plants, which are subjected to abiotic stress factors, has also been reported earlier. For instance, Liu *et al.* (Citation, 2010) reported that pretreatment of two cucumber varieties with H_2O_2 improved osmotic stress resistance by activating antioxidant system. However, to the best of our knowledge, there is little information available on the effects of H_2O_2 pretreatment on metabolite levels including soluble sugars, proline, and polyamines and ABA content in plants under osmotic stress. Exogenous H_2O_2 alone increased leaf water potential, abscisic acid (ABA) concentration and metabolite levels including soluble sugars, proline, and polyamines while it decreased lipid peroxidation and stomatal conductance. H_2O_2 pretreatment also induced the metabolite accumulation and improved water status, stomatal conductance, lipid peroxidation, ABA, and H_2O_2 levels under osmotic stress.

Table 6.6: Application of Hydrogen peroxide on different crops

PBR	Crop	Concen- tration	Type of stress	Mode of application	Effect observed	Reference
Hydrogen peroxide	Cucumber	1.5mM	Osmotic stress	Foliar spray	Increased enzy- matic antioxi- dant activities and reduced oxidative stress	Liu *et al.*, (2010)
	Soybean	1mM	Drought	Foliar spray	Increased water content and improved photosynthetic efficiency	Ishibashi *et al.*, (2011)
	Wheat	0.05μM	Salt	In nutrient solution	Increased enzy- matic antioxi- dant activities and reduced oxidative stress	Li *et al.*, (2011)

F. Abscisic acid (ABA)

Water stress affects ABA biosynthesis, leading to its accumulation. Water stress substantially accumulates ABA in a number of plant species including horticultural crops such as tomato, French bean, onion, etc. The enzyme NCED is proposed to be a key enzyme in ABA accumulation. The amount accumulated depends upon factors such as severity of stress, cultivar, species, tissue and the developmental stage. The increased ABA content plays an important role in stress tolerance following its action on stomatal regulation, root-shoot communication, induction in stress proteins and associated genes, osmolyte synthesis, senescence-promotion thereby reducing plant water use, and on maintenance of the antioxidant pool. ABA concentrations are considered a vital tool in selection and breeding of varieties for drought tolerance.

Drought stress induces stomatal closure in the leaves of many plant species. Using this mechanism, plants are able to restrict water loss through transpiration. This response is associated with decline in leaf turgor and/or water potential. Further, this regulatory mechanism is found to be linked more to the soil moisture content than to leaf water status, thereby suggesting that stomata are responsive to chemical signals produced by dehydrating roots. Sensitivity of the stomata to ABA varies widely in different species and cultivars, and, is dependent upon leaf-age, temperature, ambient CO_2 concentration, plant nutritional status, ionic status of xylem sap and leaf-water status. The ABA increase in guard cells reduces plant water loss through transpiration by promoting stomatal closure.

Several investigators have reported that shoot growth is more inhibited in plants experiencing water stress than is root growth. Some studies have also found faster root growth in limited soil water environment. Inhibition of shoot growth and increase in root weight under stress cannot be explained in terms of reduction in photosynthesis, water or nutrient supply. Investigations have revealed the association of ABA in the process by which root weight increases in response to water stress.

6.7 Conclusion

Endogenous growth regulators are vital components of plant growth and development under water stress conditions. Several reports have shown that water stress alters the level of growth regulators, and the resulting balance of growth regulators helps in providing better stress adaptability to plants through their effect on stomatal functioning, plant water-balance and growth manipulation. There is either increase or decrease in the level of growth regulators in plants under stress. While stressed plants invariably show an increase in ABA and a decrease in cytokinin, the effects of stress on ethylene and polyamines in plants are variable. Exogenous plant bio-regulator (PBR) treatment has been used to effectively improve crop drought tolerance and preserve yield under drought stress owing to their advantages of low cost, convenience, strong field operability, and/or environmental friendliness. Research efforts so far have centred on the crop and agro-ecosystem specificity, optimal doses and schedule of their application for optimizing crop yields under stress conditions. These efforts are being complemented by investigations on genes and gene regulatory network at molecular level to tailor crop plants for climate resilience.

References

Agarwal, S and Gehlot, H. S. 2000. An update on brassinosteroids. p.149-178. In: Advances in Plant Physiology, Vol. 3, Hemantarajan, A. (ed.), Scientific Publisher, India

Galuszka, P., Frebort, I., Sebela, M., Sauer, P., Jacobsen, S and Pec, P. 2001. Cytokinin oxidase or dehydrogenase? Mechanism of cytokinin degradation in cereals. Eur. J. Biochem., 268:450-461

Gao, X. P., Pan, M .J., Li, M. J., Zhang, L.Y., Wang, X. F., Shen, Y. Y., Lu, Y. F., Chen, S. W., Liang, Z and Zhang, D. P. 2004. Abscisic acid is involved in the water stress induced betaine accumulation in pear leaves. Pl. Cell Physiol., 45:742-750

Lemichez, E., Wu, L., Sanchez, J. P., Mettouchi, A., Mathur, J and Chua, N. H. 2001. Inactivation of AtRac1 by abscisic acid is essential for stomatal closure. Genet. Dev., 15:1808-1816.

Liu, K., Fu, H., Bei, Q and Luan, S. 2000. Inward potassium channel in guard cells as a target for polyamine regulation of stomata movements. Pl. Physiol., 124:1315-1326

Liu, J. H., Kitashiba, H., Wang, J., Ban, Y and Moriguchi, T. 2007. Polyamines and their ability to provide environmental stress tolerance to plants. Pl. Biotechnol., 24:117-126

Murti, G. S. R and Upreti, K. K 2000. Plant hormones. p. 109-148. In: Advances in Plant Physiology, Vol. 3, Hemantaranjan, A. (eds.) Scientific Publishers, India.

Prakash, M and Ramachandran, K. 2000. Effects of moisture stress and anti-transpirants on leaf chlorophyll. J. Agron. Crop Sci., 184:153-156

Sankhla, N., Sankhla, D., Upadhyaya, A and Davies, T.D. 1989. Amelioration of drought and high temperature injury in fruits of ber by paclobutrazol. Acta Hort., 239:197-20

Sharma, N., Abrams, S. R and Waterer, D. R. 2005. Uptake, movement, activity and persistence of an abscisic acid analog (8' acetylene ABA methyl ester) in marigold and tomato. J. Pl. Growth Regul., 24:28-35

Unyayar, S., Keles, Y and Unal, E. 2004. Proline and ABA levels in the sunflower genotypes subjected to water stress. Bulg. J. Pl. Physiol., 30: 34-47

Upreti, K. K and Murti, G. S. R. 2004c. Effect of brassinosteroids on growth, nodulation, phytohormones content and nitrogenase activity in French bean under water stress. Biol. Plant., 48:407-411

Upreti, K. K and Murti, G. S. R. 2005. Water stress induced changes in common polyamines and abscisic acid in French bean. Ind. J. Pl. Physiol., 10:145-150

7

Climate Resilient Strategies for Water Management

7.1 Introduction

Water is one of the most essential natural resources of the planet. Water is also the most critical resource for sustainable development in most of the developing countries. The quantities that are needed for drinking and sanitation purpose of humans are relatively small, and much larger quantities of water are required for many other purposes. It is essential not only for agriculture, industry and economic growth of a country, but also it is the most important component of the environment and ecosystem, with significant impact on overall wealth and nature conservation. Agricultural and industrial activities critically depend on a sufficient amount of fresh water that is withdrawn from rivers, lakes and groundwater aquifers. Currently, the rapid growth of world population along with the extension of irrigation dependent agriculture, development of industrial sector and climate change are stressing the quantity and quality of the natural water systems. Due to the increasing problems, human have begun to realize that they can no longer follow "use and discard" methodology either with water resources or any other natural resources. As a result, the need for water management has become evident. Climate change has already started to affect the hydrological cycle and the availability of freshwater for agriculture. So, proper water management practices play crucial roles in the food production and the management of ecosystems. Over the last century global irrigated area has increased more than sixfold from approximately 40 million hectares in 1900 to more than 260 million hectares in 2000. Today more than 40% of the world's food comes from the irrigated cropland which is 18% of the total cultivated crop land. Irrigated area is increased by almost 1% every year and the demand for irrigation water will increase by 13.6% by 2025 (Jensen, 1993). On the other hand about 8-15% of fresh water supply will be diverted from agricultural sector to meet the increased demand of domestic and industrial use. On the other hand the efficiency of irrigation is very low, only 65% of the applied water is used by the crop (Fig. 1). So, to overcome shortage of irrigation water for agriculture, it is essential to increase the water use efficiency in the crop field and to use marginal water for irrigation.

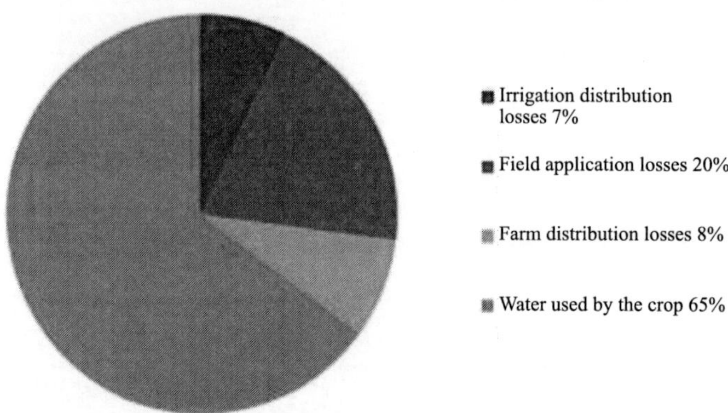

Fig. 7.1: Water losses in agriculture

7.2 Water management and climate change

According to the Intergovernmental Panel on Climate Change (IPCC, 2007), climate change is a significant threat to all nations, in particular, developing nations that are dependent on agriculture for subsistence. Climate change appears as an additional threat to water security because changes in rainfall and other climatic variables due to climate change leads to significant changes in fresh water supply in many regions (6-11). However, the effect of climate change on water resources is uncertain for different reasons. Observed data and a number of climate projections show that changes in water quantity and quality due to climate change are expected to impact negative affect on food security and increase the vulnerability of poor farmers, especially in arid and semi-arid regions. In many countries, agricultural production is already being adversely affected by climate change (FAO, 2016a). Higher temperature, less supply of water, more frequent occurrence of droughts and floods are likely to reduce yields in many areas. However, there are many non-climatic factors such as expanding population and urbanization, increasing competition for natural resources, improvement in agronomic management practices, technological innovations, global economic growth, trade and food prices that strongly influence agricultural production. These non-climatic factors have more instant impacts on water resources than those caused by climate change (Bates *et al.*, 2008). For this reason, it is more important to understand the current status of water management before assessing the impacts of climate change. From agricultural water supplies to flood management and ecosystem protection, climate change is affecting all aspects of water resource management. Rising average air temperature, loss of snowpack, frequency of flood events and rising sea level are some of the impacts of climate change that have broad implication for water resource management.

7.3 Water and agricultural production

Currently about 70% of the total water used in agriculture is mainly applied for irrigation. Although irrigation has been practiced from the ancient era, most of the irrigated lands were introduced in the 20th century. In the 1980s, the global rate of increase in irrigated area slowed considerably due to high cost of irrigation system construction, depletion of irrigation water, soil salinization and the problems of environmental protection. However, as the world population is increasing at a rapid rate, irrigation has an important role in increasing land use efficiency. Thus, in the future, irrigated farming is expected to expand rapidly with subsequent increase of water demand for irrigation.

Irrigation is not sustainable if water supply is not reliable, especially in the areas where water scarcity is the major problem for development of irrigation. So, extra Effort is needed to find economically suitable crops which can grow using minimal water, to use management practices that can minimize losses of water by evaporation from the soil and percolation of water beyond the depth of root zone and also to minimize losses of water from storage and delivery systems. Nowadays, during a period of dramatic changes in uncertainty of the water resources there is a need to provide encouragement and support to farmers to move from their traditional high-water demand cropping system and irrigation practices to modern technologies, less water demanded cropping systems.

Under scarcity of available water considerable efforts have been devoted over time to introduce different policies aiming to increase water use efficiency based on the assertion that can be achieved using less water through better management practices. Better management practices usually refer to improvement of allocate and irrigation water efficiency. The former is related to adequate pricing, while the latter depends on the type of irrigation method, timing of water application and prevailing weather condition. The yield response curve of any specific crop depends on various factors, such as weather condition, soil type and the reduction in the agricultural inputs like fertilizers and pesticides (Fig. 2). Therefore, it is difficult for a farmer to tell whether the yield loss is due to water deficit or not. Over-irrigation can cause water-logging condition for the crop, loss of nutrients due to leaching or deep percolation, contamination of the aquifers from washout agrochemicals, favourable environment for development of diseases, reduction of crop yield, increase in production cost also can create temporal water shortage to other farmers.

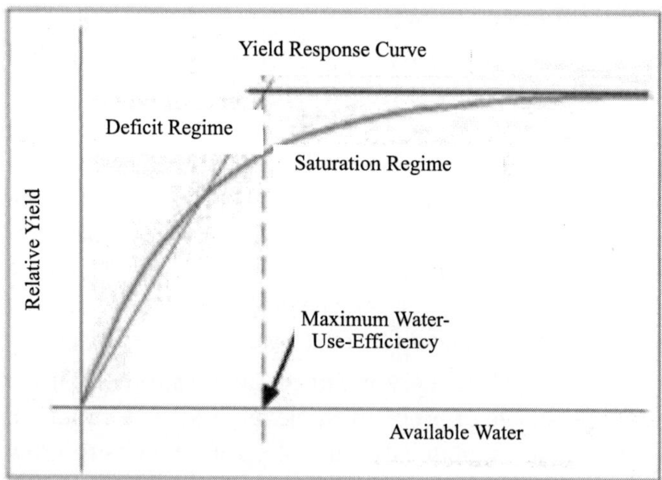

Fig. 7.2: Plant yield response to water

7.4 Water management in agriculture

Water management in agriculture aims to match water needs and water availability in quality and quantity, in space and time, at reasonable cost and with acceptable environmental impact. Its adoption depends on social behaviour and economic constrains of rural communities, legal and institutional framework, agricultural practices and technological problems.

Under water management practices most attention is given to irrigation scheduling (when to irrigate and how much water to apply) giving minor importance to irrigation method (how to apply the water in the field). Many parameters like climatic condition, water availability in the soil, crop growth stage and its sensitivity to water stress determine irrigation frequency (when to irrigate). However, the frequency depends on the irrigation method and both irrigation scheduling and irrigation method are inter-related.

7.5 Localized irrigation

Localized irrigation is widely used as one of the most efficient methods of irrigation (Keller and Bliienser, 1990). Localized irrigation systems such as trickle or drip irrigation, micro-sprayers apply the water to individual plants by plastic pipes usually laid on the ground surface. With drip irrigation system water is applied through small emitter openings from plastic pipes with a slow discharge rate of ≤ 12 l/h). With micro-sprayer or micro-sprinkler irrigation system water is sprayed over the crop plants with a discharge rate 12 to 200 l/h. The aims behind the localized irrigation are mainly the application of water directly into the root zone under the condition of low water availability, the avoidance of water losses during or after water application and the reduction of the water application cost because of less labour requirement.

Studies in diverse countries like India, United States, Israel and Spain have shown that drip irrigation can reduce water use by 30 to 70% and raises crop yield almost by 20 to 90% (Postel *et al.,* 2001). Combination of water saving and higher yield typically increases the water use efficiency at least by 50% that makes drip irrigation system a leading technology in the global challenge of increasing crop production in the face of climate change and serious water scarcity. Although the area under localized irrigation has expanded 50 times over the last two decades, it still represents less than 6% of the world's total irrigated area. The main reasons to its less expansion are the initial high investment cost (ranging from 1500 to 2500 € per hectare) and the high sensitivity to clogging.

Improvements in localized irrigation aiming to reduce the volume of water applied and increase the water use efficiency, the use of micro-sprayers in the soils having high infiltration rate, the adjustment of timing and duration of water application according to the soil and crop characteristics, the control of pressure and discharge variations, the use of appropriate filters and emitters, the adoption of proper maintenance, automation, chemigation (easy control of weeds and soil borne diseases) and fertigation (efficient fertilizer application).

7.6 Irrigation scheduling

Irrigation scheduling is a decision-making process for deciding when to irrigate the crops and how much water to apply. It forms the sole means for conserving water and it is the key to improve the performance and sustainability of the irrigation systems. It requires good knowledge about the water requirements of the crops and the characteristics of soil and crops that determines when to irrigate and how much water to apply (Fig. 3). In most of the cases, the farmer's skill determines the effectiveness of the irrigation scheduling at the field level. By adopting appropriate irrigation scheduling runoff, deep percolation and leaching out of fertilizers out of the crop root zone can be controlled, water logging can be avoided, water and energy saving can be done as less water is used, higher yield can be obtained and rising of saline water table can also be avoided. Irrigation scheduling is more important in water scarce regions than under condition of abundant water, since any excess use of water is a potential cause for deficit for other uses or users.

Irrigation techniques and tools vary greatly and have different characteristics relative to their applicability and effectiveness. Timing and depth of irrigation scheduling can be decided by using several approaches based on measurement of soil water, soil water balance and plant stress indicators in combination with different models. However, many of these models need further developments before they can be used in practice. Most of them require technical support by extension programmes, extension workers and technological expertise of the farmers. However, still in most of the countries these programmes do not exist because they are expensive, trained extension workers are lacking, farmer's knowledge and awareness of water saving in irrigation is not enough and the institutional mechanisms developed for irrigation management give low priority to the actual farming systems. Therefore, large limitations occur for their use in the farmers' practices. A brief description of irrigation scheduling techniques is reported below.

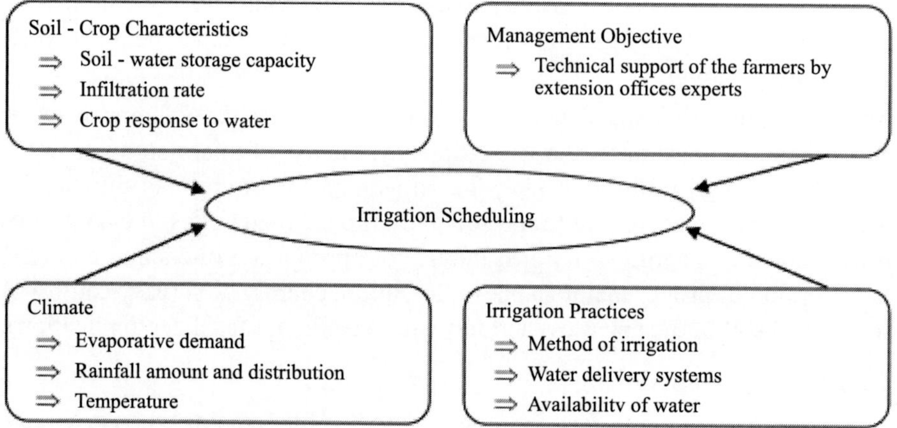

Fig. 7.3: Irrigation scheduling components

7.7 Soil water estimates and measurements

Soil water affects plant growth directly through its controlling effect on plant water status. There are two ways to measure the availability of soil water for the plants: by measuring the soil water content and soil water potential (how strongly soil water is retained in the soil). The accuracy of the information depends on the sampling methods and to the selection of location. Soil water estimates and measurements used for irrigation scheduling include: measurement of soil water content and soil water potential with tensiometer, soil spectrometers or pressure transducers, soil appearance and feel, remotely sensed soil moisture.

7.8 Crop stress parameters

Instead of estimating or measuring the soil water parameters, it is possible to receive a signal from the plants itself indicating the time of irrigation. This message can either come from an individual plant tissue (where a correct sampling is required) or from the whole canopy. Crop stress parameters include canopy temperature, leaf water content and leaf water potential, sap flow measurement, changes in stem or fruit diameter and crop stress identified by remote sensing (Deumier *et al.*, 1996; Itier *et al.,* 1993).

7.9 Weather parameters

Local or regional weather parameters are widely used for scheduling irrigation. Weather data and empirical equations that are locally calibrated are used to estimate accurate reference evapotranspiration (ET_0) for a given area and then crop evapotranspiration (ET_c) is estimated using appropriate crop coefficient according to the crop growth stage for a particular crop. On the basis of the crop evapotranspiration rate irrigation scheduling is done. This technique reduces the excess use of water.

7.10 Soil- water balance

The aim of soil water balance approach is to measure the water content in the crop root zone by water conservation equation: Δ (AWC × Root depth) = Balance of entering + outgoing water fluxes, where AWC is the available water content. Climate data, soil and crop characteristics are used to produce typical irrigation scheduling calendars by sophisticated models. This approach can be applied for individual farms and also for large regional irrigation schemes. However, it needs expert persons, support by extension services and link with information systems. Its effectiveness is high and depends on technological development and support services of the farm. Some examples of commercial software based on soil-water balance approach for irrigation scheduling are IMS (Hess, 1996), SIMIS (FAO, 1999b). MARKVAND, SALTMED (Ragab, 2002).

7.11 Effective irrigation scheduling

It is proved that appropriate irrigation scheduling can lead to improvement in irrigation water use efficiency, especially at farm level. The farmers should control the timing and the depth of irrigation. However, the practical application of the irrigation methods has been far below expectation. The main constrains to effective implementation of crop-based and water-saving irrigation scheduling are the lack of flexibility either due to rigid scheduling or the system limitations, the high cost of irrigation scheduling (cost for technology and labour covers more than 30% of the total), the lack of education and training about the irrigation management among the farmers, the lack of interactive communication between researchers, extension workers and farmers and finally the lack of demonstration and technology transfer. One of the major obstacles to effective irrigation scheduling is the inability of delivery systems to deliver water at the farm with the flexibility and reliability required. In modern irrigation networks, water is available only on demand basis, although discharge may be limited due to technical or economic reasons. The farmers are free to select and adopt the irrigation methods which they consider more appropriate to their crops and farm conditions. However, in case of limited water supply or drought, proper effective irrigation scheduling must be minted to check excess water use. Finally, government and different agencies are making effort to disseminate knowledge, upgrade training at all levels, transfer technology, incite decision-makers to changes.

7.12 Fertigation

The application of fertilizers through irrigation water is called fertigation which has become a common practice in modern agriculture. Localized irrigation systems which are highly efficient for water application, are also quite suitable for fertigation. The soluble fertilizers at required concentrations are applied through the irrigation system to the soil. But there are some disadvantages which include the non-uniform chemical distribution when irrigation designs are not adequate and the over-fertilization when irrigation is not based on actual crop requirement.

7.13 Deficit irrigation practices

In the past, irrigation scheduling did not consider limitations of the water supplies. Then irrigation scheduling was done based on covering the full water requirements of the crops. However, in arid and semi-arid regions especially in the developing areas increasing demands for water for municipal and industrial use reduce steadily water allocation to agriculture. Thus, water availability for crops is usually becoming limited and certainly not enough to get maximum crop yields. So, irrigation strategies not based on full water requirements of crops should be adopted for more effective use of available water. Such irrigation management practices include deficit irrigation, partial root drying and subsurface irrigation.

7.14 Regulated deficit irrigation

Regulated deficit irrigation (RDI) is a strategy under which crops are allowed to sustain some water deficit and yield reduction. Under regulated deficit irrigation system, the crop plants are exposed to certain degree of water stress either during a particular growth phase or throughout the growing period. The main objectives of RDI are to increase water use efficiency (WUE) of the crop by eliminating irrigation schedules that have little impact on crop yield and to improve control on vegetative growth for improving fruit size and quality. The resulting reduction of yield may be small compared with the benefits obtained through diverting the saved water to irrigate other crops for which water would be insufficient under conventional irrigation practices.

The adoption of deficit irrigation needs appropriate knowledge on crop ET, crop response to water deficit including identification of critical crop growth stages and the economic impact of yield reduction strategies. Before implementing RDI it is necessary to know the crop yield response to water deficit during a particular growth stage or whole period. Crop yield response to deficit irrigation is explained by the equation $Y/Y_m = 1\text{-}K_y\ [1\text{-}ET_a/ET_m]$ (Stewart *et al.*, 1977), where Y and Y_m are the expected and maximum crop yield, ET_a and ET_m are the actual and maximum ET, and K_y is the crop response factor. K_y gives an indication of whether the crop is tolerant to water stress and it depends on crop species, variety, growth stage and irrigation method. High yielding varieties are more sensitive to water stress. Crops or varieties with short growing periods are more suitable for RDI. Furthermore, to ensure successful RDI, the water retention capacity of the soil should also be considered. RDI must be applied during the period when shoot growth is rapid and fruit growth is slow. RDI can be applied successfully for row crops like potato, maize, soybean, sugar beet, sunflower and tree crops like grapevines, citrus, peaches, olives etc.

7.15 Partial Root Drying

Partial root drying (PRD), first applied to grapevines, is a new irrigation technique that allows one half of the crop's root system to dry while the other half is irrigated. Wet and dry sides of the root system alternate on a 7-14 day cycle. During water stress grapevine's first line of defence is to close its stomata to reduce transpiration. The principal compound that regulates this response is abscisic acid (ABA). As soil water availability falls, the drying roots starts to synthesize ABA and transported it to the leaves through the transpiration stream (Loveys *et al.,* 1999). Stomata respond by reducing aperture, thereby restricting water loss. Improvement of WUE results from partial closure of stomata. Switching of the wet and dry sectors of root zone on regular basis is necessary. PRD can be successfully applied with drip irrigation and even with subsurface irrigation in grapevines and with furrow irrigation in citrus and pear.

7.16 Subsurface Drip Irrigation

Subsurface drip irrigation is a low-pressure, low volume irrigation system that uses buried tubes to supply water. The water moves out of the tubes by the soil matrix suction force. Wetting occurs around the tubes and then water moves out in the soil in all directions. The potential advantages of subsurface drip irrigation are: a) conservation of water, b) enhancement in fertilizer use efficiency, c) uniform and highly efficient application of irrigation water, d) elimination of surface infiltration problem and evaporation losses, e) flexibility in providing frequent and light irrigation, f) less weeds infestation, g) low pressure requirement for operation. The main disadvantages are: a) high cost of initial installation and b) increased possibility for clogging especially when poor quality water is used. Subsurface drip irrigation system is especially suitable for high value fruit and vegetable crops, turfs and landscapes. The tubes are installed below the soil surface either by digging the ditches or by special device pulled by the tractor. The depth of installation depends on soil characteristics and crop species ranging from 15-20 cm for vegetable crops and 30-50 cm for fruit crops.

7.17 Agricultural Practices

Different agricultural practices such as soil management, fertilizer application and disease and pest control are related with the water management in a sustainable way to reduce water losses without hampering the environment. Today agricultural practices are characterized by the abuse of fertilizers. Farmers very rarely carry out soil and plant analysis to clarify the proper quantity and type of fertilizer needed for each crop because this process increases the cost of agricultural production. Agrochemicals, such as herbicides and pesticides are also excessively used endangering the quality of the surface water and negatively affecting the environment. There are a large number of traditional and modern soil and crop management practices for water conservation (like runoff control, improvement of soil infiltration, increase water holding capacity of soil, control of soil water evaporation) and erosion control in agriculture. The soil management practices consist of:

a) **Soil surface tillage:** Shallow tillage practices are done to produce a rough soil surface which permits short time storage of the rainfall in excess to the infiltration.

b) **Contour tillage:** Soil cultivation is done and small furrows and ridges are made along the land contour that prevents runoff. This technique is also effective to control erosion and may be applied to row crops and also to small grains where field slopes are low.

c) **Conservation tillage:** No-tillage or reduced tillage is done where residues of the previous crop are kept on the soil. The crop residues act as mulch which protects the soil from direct impact of raindrops controlling crusting and sealing processes. Conservation tillage helps to maintain high organic matter level in the soil. It is also highly effective in improving soil infiltration rate and controlling soil erosion.

d) **Mulching:** Mulching with crop residues on soil surface slowdowns water flow over the field, reduces evaporation losses, improves infiltration rate and also contributes to weed control.

e) **Organic matter:** Increasing or maintaining the amount of organic matter in the upper layer of the soils provides better soil aggregation, increases water retention capacity of the soils and reduces crusting or sealing on soil surface.

f) **Fine material or hydrophilic chemicals:** Addition of fine material or hydrophilic chemicals to the coarse soils increases the water retention capacity of the soils and also controls deep percolation. Thus, water availability in the soils which have low water holding capacity is increased.

g) **Acidity control:** Acidity control of the soils by the application of lime and similarly application of gypsum to the soils with high pH favour more intensive and deep rooting, better crop development and improve soil aggregation, thus some increase in soil water availability.

h) **Weed control:** Adoption of appropriate weed control techniques is done to alleviate competition for available soil water and transpiration losses by weeds.

Recommendations for best irrigation practices

The supply of water for irrigating the crops is decreasing steadily due to competition with demands of municipal and industrial sectors. Therefore, human resources management, technology and policy innovation are needed to increase the use efficiency of the available water. Sustainable water management in agriculture can be achieved by:

a) **Reduction of water losses:** Water leakages from the water reserves should be detected via advanced technologies like telemetry systems, remote sensing, GIS etc. Old water projects experiencing water losses should be modernized and rehabilitated.

b) **Improve the efficiency of irrigation system:** Improvements in sprinkler irrigation system (efficiency up to 85%) include the correction of sprinkler spacing, use of pressure regulators, monitoring and adjustment of pressure equipment, the design for pressure variation not exceeding 20% of the average sprinkler pressure, application of irrigation during no windy periods, use of smaller spacing and large sprinkler drops, adoption of application rates smaller than the infiltration rate of the soil and proper maintenance of the system. Improvements in localized irrigation systems include reduction of the volume of water applied by using a single drip line for a double row crop to increase the water productivity, use of micro-sprayers in soils with high infiltration rate, adjustment of duration and timing of water application to soil and crop, control of pressure and discharge variations, use of appropriate filters to the water quality, adoption of automation and careful maintenance.

c) **Increase water use efficiency:** Increase in water use efficiency can be achieved with the use of localized irrigation systems by the farmers with or without subsidies, proper irrigation scheduling according to actual requirements of the crops, introduction of appropriate agronomical practices according to the climate and the application of salinity and acidity management techniques.

d) **Adoption of innovative irrigation techniques:** In regions with water scarcity, irrigation techniques not necessarily based on full crop water requirements like subsurface irrigation or regulated deficit irrigation must be adopted. Fertigation (efficient application of fertilizers) and chemigation (easy control of weeds and soil borne diseases) should also be promoted among the rural farmers.

e) **Water pricing policy:** An increasing block tariff charging system, that discourages water use levels exceeding critical water requirements of the crops, must be introduced. It will be the basis for promoting water conservation, reducing water losses and mobilizing water resources. But it could affect cropping patterns, efficiency of water management, income distribution and generation of additional revenue for operating and maintenance of water projects.

f) **Reuse of marginal waters (reclaimed or brackish) for irrigation:** Reclaimed waters can be used under some restrictions for irrigation of trees and fodder crops. Treated sewage should be looked upon with skepticism by the farmers. They instead prefer to use surface or groundwater for irrigation. Special effort is needed for educating farmers to accept treated sewage. In addition, the tariff for these sources of water should be lower than the tariff of the primary sources. This may not be difficult to achieve because the primary and secondary levels of treatment are regarded as sunk costs since they are required by the new WFD. When using low quality irrigation water like brackish or saline water an integrating approach for crop (salt tolerant varieties) field management (suitable tillage practices) and suitable irrigation system should be adopted.

g) **Wider and effective participation of the public:** Need wider and more effective participation of Government sectors and NGOs in decision-making and the preparation of water management plans, monitoring the implementation and generally in the management of water. The participation of these groups raises support on the part of the body politics and also promotes success in possible conflict resolutions.

h) **Capacity building:** The existing "capacity building" is under poor condition. It needs appropriate competent personnel, advance technologically based devices and facilities, legal guidelines, efficient administrative and effective processes for the sustainable management of the water resources. It includes:

- Education and training of professionals, technical staffs, decision makers and others including non-public organizations is necessary for sustainable water management.
- Institutions should be staffed with qualified manpower like managers, engineers, technicians etc.
- Water authorities should apply updated technologies, advanced devices and programs e.g. GIS, remote sensing etc. These advanced techniques help water managers in their decision- making.
- Water authorities should participate in the formulation of agricultural policies because the development of water and land should be fully integrated. In practice, agricultural decisions are water decisions and vice versa.

7.18 Conclusion

Climate change already starts to hamper agriculture, especially in the areas under arid and semiarid climatic regions. Thus, the reduction in rainfall and the increase in temperature cause reductions in yield and profit, as crops are impacted by water and heat stress. Under this perspective, implementation of appropriate adaptation and mitigation strategies will help to reduce these negative impacts ensuring the economic and environmental sustainability of the current agricultural system. Correct water management strategies or soil management practices of conservation agriculture are some of the measures recommended.

To identify those management strategies more suitable for each crop and location, a correct characterization of the agricultural systems will be critical. Thus, crop phenology and its sensitivity to water or heat stress, soil characteristics, availability of water resources are some knowledge requirements that must be considered for implementation of water management practices under climate change.

References

Deumier J.M., Leroy P. and Peyremorte P. (1996). Tools for improving management of irrigated agricultural crop systems. In: Irrigation Scheduling: From Theory to Practice, Proceedings ICID/FAO Workshop, Sept. 1995, Rome. Water Report No. 8, FAO, Rome.

FAO, 1999. The state of food insecurity in the world. Rome, Italy.

FAO, 1999b. Land and Water Digital Media Series no 6. (www.fao.org).

Hess T. M. (1996). A microcomputer scheduling program for supplementary irrigation. Computers and Electronics in Agriculture 15: 233 – 243.

Itier B., Flura D. and Belabess K. (1993). An alternative way for C.W.S.I. calculation to improve relative evapotranspiration estimates: results of an experiment over soybean. Acta Hortic., 335, 333-340.

Jensen M.E. (1993). The impacts of irrigation and drainage on the environment. 5th Gulhati Memorial Lecture. 15th ICID Congress, The Hague, ICID, New Delhi.

Loveys B.R., Dry P.R. and McCarthy M.G. (1999). Using plant physiology to improve water use efficiency of horticultural crops. Acta Hort. 537: 187-199.

Postel S., Polak P., Gonzales F. and Keller J. (2001). Drip irrigation for small farmers. A new initiative to alleviate hunger and poverty. Water Intern. 26 (1): 3-13.

Ragab, R. (2002). A Holistic Generic Integrated Approach for Irrigation, Crop and Field Management: The SALTMED Model. J. of Environmental Modelling & software, 17:345-361.

Stewart J.I., Cuenca R.H., Pruitt W.O., Hagan R.M. and Tosso L. (1977). Determination and utilization of water production functions on principal California crops. W-67 California Contributing Project Report, Davis, University of California, USA.